Praise for Teacher

What educator would not want to work i
However, changing the narrative about the
especially when much of what is we read are the unrelenting workloads, self-doubt, stress, and burnout teachers experience. Fortunately, Cherkowski and Walker provide a blueprint for reframing the narrative about teacher wellbeing, focusing on how growth mindsets, appreciative inquiry, hope, and resilience can sustain a flourishing school culture. Teachers and administrators who are inspired to "up their game" to thrive in schools should read and reflect on the ideas in this book.

Bruce Barnett, Professor Educational Leadership and Policy Studies
University of Texas at San Antonio

Cherkowski and Walker have tackled a very important area - the combination of theory and practical strategies about educator wellbeing make this book one to add to your professional collection.

Linda Kaser, Director of Networks of Inquiry and Innovation,
Vancouver, BC, Canada

In their book Teacher Wellbeing, Sabre Cherkowski and Keith Walker seek to transition teachers' discouragement, frustration, and even burnout into an awakening sense of wellbeing and flourishing. Such an endeavor is daunting, but not impossible, especially when in the hands of these two gifted researchers and educators. Integrating findings from positive psychology with freeing contemplative activities, they engage readers in the process of developing the skills and perspectives that will enhance their enjoyment in their work and lives. And since teachers teach themselves more than their subjects, the benefits they gain will enrich their students' wellbeing as well.

Dr. Beverly Hardcastle Stanford

This is a very helpful guide to nurturing Teacher Wellbeing. I particularly like the concept of heartprints which the authors introduce in the book to identify what touches and moves a person. We need heartprints to help teachers thrive and flourish. The book contains lots of other ideas that teachers will find helpful.

Jack Miller, Professor in the Department of Curriculum, Teaching and Learning at the University of Toronto and author of The Holistic Curriculum

This little book should be in the hands of every school leader and utilized to create a culture of wellbeing. As leaders, we are aware that we need to help create and maintain a positive culture. What we don't know is what steps to take to make that happen. This book provides a roadmap to get it done.

Jeanne L. Surface, Ed.D., University of Nebraska Omaha

This book challenges much conventional thinking about what it takes to improve schools, balancing theory from several disciplines with stories from schools and practical guidance. A refreshing addition to the literature and an uplifting read.

Dr Louise Stoll, Professor of Professional Learning,
UCL Institute of Education, London.

At a time when there is too much focus on the negative aspects of schools, this book provides inspiration for a positive and hopeful consideration of the work of educators. Cherkowski and Walker provide wisdom and insight that helps teachers and school leaders to reconsider their work from a positive perspective. Innovative guided reflections and actions throughout the book promote reader engagement. Practical, scholarly, insightful, this is a book that will be a resource for those in schools wanting to better support their colleagues, and to develop communities full of hope.

David Gurr, Associate Professor of Educational Leadership,
University of Melbourne.

The book's message is as simple as it is powerful – when teachers flourish, so do our children. The authors' messages are brought to life by research, experience and a genuine care, and this results in book which will actually work in schools. I highly recommend it to anyone seeking better, more human schools.

Allan Walker, Joseph Lau Chair Professor of International
Educational Leadership, Dean, Faculty of Education and Human
Development, Director, Asia Pacific Centre for Leadership and
Change, The Education University of Hong Kong

Within these pages, Professors Cherkowski and Walker powerfully, purposefully, and persuasively reconnect us to the idea of flourishing and well being. This important idea is grounded in the fact that the work of educators is at its core a human endeavor; a fact for far too long has been background in favor of technical and mechanistic approaches to the educative process. The authors draw on high quality research and practice delivered through clear and accessible prose that engages and delights. The text reminds us that the space in which learning takes place is a sacred one, and at its best when it is intentionally, mindfully, and compassionately nurtured. For all these reasons and so many more this book is a must read for all who care about the future of educators and education

Alan J. Daly, Professor, University of California, San Diego

Sabre and Keith have invited us to imagine workplaces in which we thrive, and that support the flourishing of the other adults and young people who inhabit these school spaces as well. They note that too many educators have become weary in their "well-doing," and thus extend an invitation for us to explore educator "wellbeing."

Megan Tschannen-Moran, Professor of Educational Policy, Planning, and Leadership at the College of William and Mary's School of Education

Thus, the enormous importance of this book's living theory of flourishing and wellbeing within a self-governing community of learners—both teacher and student. I congratulate the authors for attending to this so very important agenda.

Jerry Starratt, Professor Emeritus, Boston College

Teacher Wellbeing

Noticing, Nurturing, Sustaining, and Flourishing in Schools

Sabre Cherkowski
& Keith Walker

Teacher Wellbeing

Noticing, Nurturing, Sustaining, and Flourishing in Schools

Sabre Cherkowski
& Keith Walker

Word & Deed Publishing Inc.
1860 Appleby Line, Suite #778
Burlington, Ontario, Canada
L7L 7H7

Teacher Wellbeing:
Noticing, Nurturing, Sustaining, and Flourishing in Schools

Edited by Darrin Griffiths, Ed.D.
Book design by Jim Bisakowski – www.bookdesign.ca
Illustrations by Debbie Donsky, Ed.D. - www.debbiedonsky.com

ISBN 978-0-9959782-2-5

Word & Deed Publishing Incorporated
1860 Appleby Line, Suite #778
Burlington, Ontario, Canada, L7L 7H7
(Toll Free) 1-866-601-1213

Visit our website at
www.wordanddeedpublishing.com

Dedication

As teachers, we are grateful for those who have taught us, who continue to teach us, and who commend teaching to us as a vocation. Teaching is a high calling; a calling that both of us as authors have accepted with humility and thankfulness. We love to be identified as "teachers." The opportunity to handle the precious treasure of trust and good will, to spend time in the highly "peopled" world of education, and to learn from young and older. Teaching allows us the space to do right, to do good, to be ourselves, and to foster the best in those we learn alongside of. We dedicate this book to our students who have been our teachers and to our teachers who have imparted their *joie de vivre,* wisdom, and passion. The ones we most remember were the healthy ones who taught us to play, to work hard according to our passions and towards a higher purpose, along with those who exemplified finding pleasure in their service to others.

In particular, Sabre wishes to dedicate this book to her graduate student, Kelly Hanson, who worked with her to initially organize the ideas and practices from the research into a book format. Kelly's commitment to deep collaboration and her unwavering commitment to teacher education and growth through appreciative processes have been a source of inspiration and learning for Sabre, and for many of the participants with whom Kelly engaged as a research assistant through this journey. She also dedicates this book to her husband, Kevin and their children (Nicholas and Anne) with much love, gratitude, and appreciation for their cheerleading and support.

In particular, Keith wishes to dedicate this book to his teacher-mentors: Keith Shaw, Murray Smith, Ron Kirstein, Gene Howard, Walter Boldt, Joe Pyra, Larry Sackney, Murray Scharf, Patrick Renihan, Kabini Sanga, and, with much affection, to Viv Walker and their eight adult children, by birth and marriage (Gillian, Cody, Graham, Stacie, Eric, SJ, James, and Martha).

Sabre and Keith

Acknowledgements

Sabre and Keith wish to acknowledge the funding from the Social Sciences and Humanities Research Council of Canada that supported their research on flourishing in schools.

They would like to thank the graphic designer, Debbie Donsky, who brought their ideas to life in the living map diagram and the images sprinkled throughout the pages of the book.

Finally, Sabre and Keith express sincere and heartfelt gratitude to Darrin Griffiths for his enthusiasm for this book, his generosity as an editor, and his spirit as an educator. To our "book Butler" (as he delightfully refers to himself), we offer our deep thanks.

Contents

Foreword

As an educator who has traveled to Canada off and on over the past fifty years, for various work with Canadian educators, I have always been impressed with both the quality of scholarship productivity and also the warm sense of interpersonal community among Canadian educators. I was therefore anxious to read this gem of a book that summarizes the results of the authors' on-the-ground research and proposals for improving the human flourishing of schools.

The authors have been developing a "living theory" that names the phenomenon of flourishing schools, a theory that echoes scholarly research emerging in psychological and organizational studies of the notion of wellbeing and its positive impact on the workforce. Their field studies have surfaced very encouraging adaptations of efforts to promote a sense of individual and communal flourishing in schools through the use of "appreciative inquiry" exercises. The authors can legitimately label their research findings as generating a "living theory" in the sense that their findings are embedded in multiple, richly human narratives that portray both creative initiatives dealing with complex and diverse challenges, where teachers working in various support groups generate responses that lead to their wellbeing as they embrace creative responses to their classroom challenges.

The book illustrates the importance of attending to the hurdles teachers, including beginning teachers, face as they encounter challenges unforeseen in their university experience, leading them to doubt their capability to meet the needs expressed in their students' struggles with the social and cultural pressures of school and home. The book offers structured exercises that enable teachers to work with their personal talents and interests in their relationships with their students. The authors clearly embrace the development of "leaderful" school communities, in which veteran teachers are encouraged to support teachers with multiple, reflective discussions on how to promote student involvement in their learning so as to enable them to flourish in their school work. These supportive teacher-leaders encourage young teachers to surface small, but significant, successes they have facilitated to provide added motivation to continue to work from their growing repertory of successful pedagogies, rather than to focus on correcting negatives in their pedagogical efforts. Principal involvement with organizing these kinds of reflective exercises of "appreciative inquiry" is seen as a key leadership role for principals.

Besides attention to the practical management of stress, self–esteem, and workload issues, the authors cite examples of inspiring group reflections on the sacredness of the vocation of teaching, its attention to the sacredness of the youngsters in their charge, the significance of their work in preparing the next generation of citizens among whom will arise leaders in the arts, in politics, in engineering, in various scholarly disciplines, and among whom will be parents who raise healthy children, as well neighborhood leaders who inspire their communities. The authors single out these often neglected reflections that help them refocus on the primary value of their contribution to the wellbeing of their young learners and to their communities. Those reflection sessions can often emerge into a form of community self-governance that affect the flourishing and wellbeing of the school community.

Based on their living theory of flourishing, the authors offer flexible starting points that each school may adapt and adopt, initiatives that are more responsive to specific school communities. The book may serve as a consistent, yet flexible, guide to ongoing efforts that build on emerging strengths generated by early wellbeing development, as the school continues to stress the process of "appreciative inquiry" that encourages the continuous surfacing of successful efforts to respond to student needs. Even in situations where schools or school systems have experienced success in responding to assessments of curriculum standards, the book may provide valuable guidance to counter the exclusive emphasis on abstract statistical summaries of student scores on state and local assessments of student performances by supplying a missing, supplementary emphasis on the human development of both teachers and students. The work of teaching and learning is, after all, a human work that explores meaningful relationships between living in the worlds of nature, culture, and society, and further explores ways those meanings suggest various ways of participating in those worlds. That participation is, and will be, how humans carry on the specific adventure of sustaining and renewing a free and responsible society. The struggle teachers face is very much how—given the curriculum focus of their pedagogy—they create in their classrooms miniature worlds of culture, of nature, and of society, by which their students gain a sense of membership, and begin their participation, in those worlds.

Thus, the enormous importance of this book's living theory of flourishing and wellbeing within a self-governing community of learners—both teacher and student. I congratulate the authors for attending to this so very important agenda.

Robert J. Starratt,
Professor Emeritus
Boston College

Jerry Starratt is an internationally well-known and respected educator (teacher, principal, and professor), a favourite provocator, a compassionate and conviction-filled scholar-practitioner; he is a dear colleague and mentor to many. He and Thomas Sergiovanni helped to redefine supervision in schools; his published works and teaching on ethical and learning-centered leadership, on cultivating meaning, community, responsibility, and more democratic schools are highly valued by educators around the world.

Chapter One

Introduction

Teachers play a crucial partnership role in fostering wellbeing in their students' lives. When we read that: "a teacher affects eternity" (Henry Adams); "a great teacher is a great artist...[that] teaching might even be the greatest of the arts since the medium is the human mind and spirit" (John Steinbeck); "everyone who remembers his or her own education remembers teachers, not methods and techniques. The teacher is the heart of the education system" (Sidney Hook); "most of us end up with no more than five or six people who remember us [but] teachers have thousands of people who remember them for the rest of their lives" (Andy Rooney); as "One looks back with appreciation at the brilliant teachers, but with gratitude to those who touched our human feelings... warmth is the vital element for the growing plant and for the soul of the child" (Carl Jung); or, when we hear Temple Grandin say that "I cannot emphasize enough the importance of a good teacher," we are not or should not be surprised. Speaking of the calling of the teacher, George Steiner said: "There is no craft more privileged. To awaken another human being's powers, dreams beyond one's own; to induce in others a love for that which one loves; to make one's inward present their future; that is the threefold adventure like no other."

We join with these, and others, who resonate with our claim that teachers have vital and sacred roles in the lives of communities. Fundamentally, we believe that teacher wellbeing is linked to student and community wellbeing. Teacher wellbeing matters. Happy, healthy teachers who feel well and whole in their work provide strong support for happy, healthy children and youth. We want to encourage teachers to flourish because they, in turn, make ways for those within their circles of influences (children, youth, and their families) to flourish. We hold to the view that when human beings honour and care for one another, then there are reciprocal, or virtuous, cycles that are created. So that as healthy teachers care for others, those cared for become healthier and those who are caring receive benefits from their own well-doing. For us, the important work of developing flourishing schools can be a one-person-at-a-time call to make space for healthy teachers to provide caring support for the wellbeing of each of their students.

Learning happens best when teachers and their students are well, and know that the aggregate or composite health of all teachers, staff, and students will determine the overall wellbeing of the learning community. Knowing this, we put this call out for growing wellbeing to all teachers, and to all those who support teachers in their work, including those who formally or informally lead in schools. For us, wellbeing describes the wholeness and the aliveness of the individual and the system. Wellbeing has been described in terms of engagement, connection, meaning, positive feelings, and a sense of achievement in life (Seligman, 2011). This sense of wellbeing will be different for different people and different groups, but, in common, knowing what makes us feel whole, alive, connected, engaged, and acting with purpose in our work is essential to being able to attend to our wellbeing. We find that as teachers shift their focus toward what makes them feel well in their work, they then attend to the cognitive, social, emotional, spiritual, and physical elements and aspects that contribute to their wellbeing, and they give attention to growing more of this for themselves, and their students.

Wellbeing in schools has received international attention as researchers highlight the importance of attending to students' social- emotional learning (Cohen, 2001; Elias & Arnold, 2006; Greenberg, et al., 2003; Jennings & Greenberg, 2009), attending to their moral development through character education (Berkowitz & Bier, 2005), and awareness of students' experiences of positive affect in schooling, such as experiences with kindness and empathy (Binfet, 2015, 2016). Consistently, the role of teachers is highlighted as a key element to ensure the conditions necessary for developing students' intellectual and social-emotional capacities and capabilities (Zins, Weissberg, Wang, & Walberg, 2004).

Although we may have a vague sense that teachers make a difference in students' lives, focusing on teacher wellbeing has only recently been identified as an area of importance for researchers world-wide. For example, in a recent report prepared for the United Nations Education Scientific and Cultural Organization (UNESCO), researchers from a group of 30 Asia-Pacific countries detailed how they have been working together to determine how to establish happy schools, given the evidence of the positive connection between wellbeing and improved learning (Kim, 2016). From their qualitative research, they identified a number of factors contributing to a happy school: where students felt included, engaged, connected, and inspired to learn; where there were friendships and relationships within the school community; where there was a warm and friendly learning environment; where there was evidence of learner freedom, creativity and engagement; where teamwork and a collaborative spirit were in operation; and where there were positive teacher attitudes and attributes, including "kindness, enthusiasm and fairness, as well as an emphasis on the role of teachers in serving as inspiring, creative, and, ultimately, happy role models for learners (p. 38).

While we see clearly that teachers' wellbeing is essential for ensuring schools are happy places for students to learn and grow, we do question the singular focus for practice and policy on improving student wellbeing. Our assumption from this lack of specific attention to teacher wellbeing is that there has been an implicit understanding that teachers will take care of their own wellbeing, given the importance of this for their students. We are convinced that this assumption needs to change; we need to consciously attend to and support teacher wellbeing in similar ways that we are attending to student wellbeing in schools.

In other places, we also see the recent promotion and support of teacher wellbeing in schools among educational stakeholders. For example, in the United Kingdom, the National Union of Teachers has drawn attention to the alarming rates of teacher stress and burnout, pointing to the need for significant changes to reduce excessive workload demands and toxic work environments for teachers brought about by stringent accountability-driven assessment measures (NUT, nd). Moreover, researchers Greenberg, Brown and Abenavoli (2016) issued a report about teacher stress in the United States and urged for more attention on organizational and individual interventions to help reduce stress and promote wellbeing for teachers, stating that this is a national crisis.

The research on current practices provides mounting evidence that we need more resources and attention to how we might effectively support teachers through the stress of this sacred and taxing work they do. Given that teachers are the strongest factor of influence on student achievement in the classroom (Hattie, 2008), and that teachers' well-being contributes to fostering happy schools where students can thrive (Kim, 2016), it makes sense that we spend considerable time and serious attention to ensure that teachers are well in their work settings. Right now, however, there are too many teachers who are suffering. This is due, in part, to our—and their own—neglect of the importance of noticing, nurturing, and sustaining their wellbeing. Stress, exhaustion, burnout, uncertainty, anxiety, isolation, despair—these are the all-too-real and pervasive descriptors for how many teachers are feeling in, and about, their work (Fernet, Guay, Seneccal & Austin, 2012; Bermejo-Toro, Prieto-Ursua & Hernandez, 2016; Greenberg, Brown & Abenavoli, 2016). Too many of our teacher colleagues across the world suffer from sources of stress that put an enormous strain on their ability to feel well in their work. This situation also invades their personal and familial lives in ways that can be devastating. We know that many teachers suffer from working in negative, damaged, or toxic school environments. Some experience relentless job demands, and others have too few resources and too little support available to carry out their work. Teachers also suffer from strains and stresses emerging from insufficient personal levels of social-emotional competency (Greenberg et al., 2016).

With all of this suffering (often silent and profound), it is no wonder that teachers are struggling under the weight of chronic stress at work. Of course, teachers can become weary in their well-doing. Teachers can be worn down by the daunting tasks afforded them. We know from our own work with teachers that the work of teaching, learning, and leading in schools is increasingly felt to be an impossible job; one where meeting the seemingly relentless myriad of change demands and reforms that are thrown at teachers and administrators dismisses and displaces their energies. These pressures and burdens can effectively create a greater and greater gulf between what teachers have always aimed to do in their work—meet students' needs in responsive, creative, and loving ways—and what they are often tasked to do in schools—carry out teaching plans that satisfy the incessant need for standardized performance and accountability-driven policies. It is not surprising that teachers experience high levels of stress, and that this, in turn, leads to increased anxiety, frustration, desperation, and, eventually, burnout.

We reject the "survival of the fittest," or the "so it has always been," views that are passive or indifferent to the challenges faced by teachers. Any thoughts of minimizing or ignoring the inherent vocational dangers of teaching will only result in leaving teachers to languish and become beleaguered, and this is not acceptable. Teachers warrant our moral and practical support and attention. Through our research and writing, we argue strongly for schools and school systems to orient their attitudes, resources, and structures toward wellbeing for all—and certainly for teacher wellbeing.

However, we also want to be clear that we do not think we can wait for the structural, political, and economic pieces to fall into place to ensure that teachers have what they need for the self-care required for their wellbeing at work. Teachers need to be encouraged, exhorted, and empowered to take care of themselves, and each other, in order that they might effectively continue to foster good in the lives of others. Through this book, we offer our encouragement toward what we hope will become opportunities for teacher empowerment for attending to their own sense of flourishing, despite the very real conditions we have described that can make it challenging for teachers to feel well at work.

We recognize that in some jurisdictions there are fewer expressions of hyper-rationalized, standardized, and accountability-driven forms of education; but, there are plenty of other pressures that accumulate to burden teachers and threaten their adaptive systems. The demands on teachers are great, and the support for ensuring their wellbeing so that they can carry out their work in an engaged and motivated way has always been a challenge (Apple & Beane, 2007; Giroux, 2015; Giroux & McClaren, 1989). For example, there are international shifts toward new ways of deep learning that encourage and promote competencies for 21st Century learners that are necessitating significant changes for many teachers; such shifts in practice require new ways of professional learning and collaborative engagement with colleagues. The demands on teachers to develop new competencies and capacities such that they are able to learn in collaborative ways with their colleagues and to provide deep and meaningful learning for their students are real, and, yet, we wonder if there has been serious enough consideration of the structural, organizational, and professional support required for teachers to undertake these new challenges in their work. As we learn from the growing trends in the described (above) research, and as we ponder our own long-standing research with teachers to understand what it means to flourish in schools, the focus on teachers' wellbeing remains an essential pillars for our encouragement and support for new structures, practices and mindsets for new ways of teaching.

Turning Toward a New Story of Teaching—Flourishing

We don't mean to indicate that only through future intent toward wellbeing will teachers flourish. Already, teachers can and do thrive. There are "on-the-ground teachers" who have witnessed sustained flourishing in their own work lives, and in the lives of others. We think their stories provide warranted hope in the context of educational circumstances that have been described as volatile, uncertain, complex, and ambiguous (VUCA). Building a new story with—and from—teachers about what it means to thrive in their work has been our passion over the last several years. We believe that teachers deserve to think of their work, and themselves in their work, as worthy of flourishing. When they do, this can prompt positive changes in how they act and feel, both in their work and in their lives in general. While "flourishing" has philosophical and psychological roots, we want to grow educators' own theories for this word; to make the notion come to life for them as a central component of a story that highlights the joy, purpose, fun, and engagement that can be experienced through teaching. We acknowledge the challenges, suffering, and heartache that can come with being called to teach. While we don't have, nor do we aim to develop, one single definition of flourishing for teachers, we do know that our understanding includes approaching the work of teaching from a different and affirming mindset; one that orients us more often toward noticing our work from a positive, strengths-based, appreciative perspective.

What does it mean to propose a shift in the mindset of teachers, as a way to re-story their work toward flourishing? A mindset is "a belief that biases how you think, feel, and act. It's like a filter through which you see everything through. Not every belief can become a mindset... the beliefs that become mindsets transcend preferences, learned facts, or intellectual opinions. They are core beliefs that reflect your philosophy of life" (McGonigal, 2015, p. 11). Mindset researchers have argued that we can shift how we feel and act by shifting our thinking, and that this can create new mindsets (Dweck, 2006; McGonigal, 2015). Too often we think about the stories about teacher stress, exhaustion, and burnout, which has led us to wonder about an alternate story about teaching, a new mindset about what it means to teach, learn, and lead in schools from an appreciative, generative, and positive perspective.

We've wondered, out loud and to ourselves, about how schools and people in schools flourish. Ideas about human flourishing, once the purview of philosophy, have crossed disciplines and are being taken up in research in psychology and organizational studies. As life-long teachers, we've purposed to bring ideas from the disciplines of positive psychology and positive organization studies into the field of education to explore flourishing in schools. Through our research connections with teachers and school administrators we are working to develop a definition of flourishing applied to education; one that honours the work of teaching, learning, and leading in schools, that recognizes the complexity of that work, and that highlights a holistic understanding of teacher wellbeing as deeply connected to the success and wellbeing of students. Teachers feel a sense of flourishing when their students are flourishing. However, that sense of flourishing is not boundless. There are conditions, forces, and factors that play into what it means to flourish as a teacher. For example, teachers who flourish experience meaningful collaborative relationships with their colleagues, and feel that they are working toward a common purpose in serving their students. They find opportunities to connect with their colleagues in laughter, in enjoyment of their work, and in other aspects of their lives. They feel sufficiently supported by their administrators to engage in adapting and responding in their work for their students (Cherkowski & Walker, 2016; Cherkowski, Hanson & Walker, 2018).

We have suggested that gaining and maintaining wellbeing at work is an individual's responsibility; at the same time, we also suggest that flourishing in schools is an organizational imperative in which teachers, administrators, district leaders, and community partners all need to be engaged together in the pursuit of everyone's wellbeing. For us, part of what it means to flourish is to recognize that the pursuit of wellbeing acknowledges and honours the intricately interdependent nature of a living system, where unique needs of individuals and common needs of the systems often overlap, and where there is a sense of aiming to cooperate to have all needs met in ways that grow the individuals and the system (Capra, 2004; Hargreaves & Fink, 2006; Wheatley, 1999).

We want to be clear that while we argue for the need to highlight and support the wellbeing of teachers, students, and all members of the learning community, as an essential pillar for organizing schools, we do not think that individuals should wait to flourish until their organizations, and those who work with them in these systems, pay attention to wellbeing. Instead, we suggest that teachers can enable themselves at any moment to prioritize their own wellbeing and move, in small ways, towards flourishing. It can be a choice to initiate and support a mindset shift. We agree with McGonigal (2015) who argued that "one of the most helpful mindset shifts you can make is to view yourself as the source of whatever support you want to experience" (p. 173). Yes, it may be more difficult in some schools than in others for teachers to intentionally focus on their wellbeing; however, we think that the theory and practice that we offer in this book can be a starting point, or place of encouragement, to give teachers small opportunities for shifting how they nurture their wellbeing as a priority in their work. We have learned through our research with teachers that flourishing can be framed as an option, a choice for each individual teacher at any time (Cherkowski, Hanson & Walker, 2018). Of course, typically it is easier to attain and sustain wellbeing in an organization that is healthy and supportive, but we repeat that this does not mean that teachers must wait for schools to move toward supporting flourishing before they, themselves, can notice, nurture, and sustain their own sense of flourishing. As we will see, wellbeing is not part of a binary system (either you are well or you are ill); but, rather, wellbeing is a condition or state on a continuum with a number of dimensions and features.

Teachers' flourishing in schools is a personal, interpersonal, and organizational responsibility. As teachers move toward flourishing they will notice that their relationships with their students, colleagues, and the larger learning community become more positive—and perhaps even more fun. They find that they look forward to their work, and they find that they have more energy and enthusiasm to collaborate with their colleagues. They find that interactions at meetings become more thoughtful and meaningful. They notice students engaging in more kind and caring ways. And they find that those they work with have more energy and enthusiasm for their learning, and that they delight in the learning experienced by those around them. As with all dynamic systems, influences and disturbances can create reciprocal shifts across other areas, and we suggest that positive disturbances can shift a system in the same way as negative ones can. In her research on stress, McGonigal (2015) noted the significant physical changes that can ensue from shifting mindsets toward the positive benefits and possibilities that can emerge from stressful situations, not just ruminating on the negative aspects. We understand from positive psychology that humans tend to have a negativity bias. As people tend to respond more quickly and with more energy to negative disruptions, this means that the exercise of positive influence has to work harder to get the same reactions that the negative initiatives do (Cameron, 2008). This is important to know, as we hope to influence positive shifts in organizations. We have to maintain purposeful attention to positive, appreciative ways of working and influencing to ensure that the positive changes gain—and maintain—traction. Is this likely to happen quickly? Not necessarily. However, from our conversations with teachers and other school leaders, we have seen how a shift toward positive, appreciative, and generative mindsets can provide a positive catalyst for promoting similar shifts among their students and others in their school.

We've learned that joining with others as part of the journey, a journey toward growing and sustaining wellbeing for self and others, is a meaningful and powerful experience. Throughout this book we offer theory and practice for individuals, teams, and entire organizations to notice, nurture, and sustain flourishing for self and others. We see this shift toward developing and maintaining positive school organizations as an essential pillar in attaining school improvement goals for ensuring that all students in all schools experience learning opportunities for them to flourish in the present, and into their futures.

We are interested in learning about and sharing processes for measuring, fostering, and sustaining flourishing in schools. One of our guiding questions has been, "What are the factors, forces, and dynamics that interact to explain how it is that certain schools and certain people in schools flourish?" Over the course of this flourishing-in-schools research, we aimed to establish an inventory of the conditions, catalysts, and galvanizing forces that seem to characterize flourishing for people in schools. We've wondered what a toolkit of instruments to identify and measure flourishing in schools might look like, and we offer this book as one piece of what we hope will be an emergent and ongoing development of tools, strategies, and resources for growing teacher wellbeing. We have thoroughly enjoyed working with others who share our passion for growing wellbeing as a central focus in education. Through this book, we share with you our knowledge and practices about teacher wellbeing and flourishing in schools, and invite you into our network of learning about teacher wellbeing. We hope that you will reach out and connect with other colleagues to grow your part of this network; perhaps you will even connect with us, whether as educator, researcher, learner, person in an allied human services profession, or as a person of skills and insights who simply is interested in coming along for the ride.

This book is organized to guide your inquiry toward growing your awareness, capabilities, and capacities for journeying toward flourishing for yourself and others in your work in schools. This book is a compilation of what we have learned as we researched what it means to flourish in schools, and so we use pieces of our own published research articles, as well as our interpretations of other current research and writing in education, psychology, business, and other disciplines, to offer just enough theory to add to your own in order to help inform and shape your inquiry. We provide stories and anecdotes from our lives—and from our participants' lives and experiences—to animate and enliven the ideas that we are sharing. We also offer moments of pause that allow you to rest, reflect, and make sense of what you're reading in ways that affirm the essence of who you are as a teacher, and that encourage and inspire you to stretch toward a greater sense of wholeness and wellbeing in your work and life. We call these moments ***Heart Prints.*** We provide moments of creative activity that serve to shift the ground a little, to perhaps even shake things up for you or provoke you. We call these moments ***Shifting Ground.*** You will find examples of these moments woven throughout the book. Our hope is that you can use this book to inform your thinking, to affirm the steps you've already been taking toward greater wellbeing, and to offer a chance to build up and work towards developing your own theory of flourishing.

Although we believe that gaining wellbeing is an organizational imperative, we also know that real change happens when individuals feel challenged to shift their mind, heart, and habits, and that this often happens in a safe, supportive, and caring environment. This book is intended to be that environment. We offer up a gentle and contemplative text that challenges you to think and act in new ways; in ways that nourish you, and also in ways that help you to feel that you are having a conversation with caring colleagues who aim to support you.

If you have a propensity to action, we hope that you will take time to reflect on your own personal and professional development. We encourage you to document your learning in the spaces we provide for you, or in any other ways that you prefer, to help you to best make meaning of your experiences as you read through the book.

We have organized this book using four signals of teachers and schools who thrive —**noticing, nurturing, sustaining, and flourishing.** Early in our research journey our goal was to provide clear concepts for our participants in terms of how they might share with us their stories about what it means for them to flourish in their work. As we progressed, these four signals emerged for us, and we believe they provide a guide for those interested in inquiring into their flourishing at personal, team, or organizational levels. For example, a teacher (or team or whole school or district) could intentionally focus on *noticing* where they feel a sense of flourishing in their work, and documenting what they find as a way of capturing experiences and moments where they feel well, engaged, alive, and purposeful in their work. They could then determine what they might want to do to *nurture* and grow this sense of flourishing through structuring their work in certain ways, connecting more frequently with certain people, and accessing resources that seem to promote their wellbeing. They might work on their own, and with their colleagues, to establish structures, habits, celebrations, ceremonies, relationships, and other dynamics for *sustaining* this sense of flourishing for themselves, and for others the school.

There have been positive responses from teachers and other school leaders who have spoken to us about the usefulness of these signals in helping to establish guideposts for how to focus on wellbeing in their work. We do not assume that these signals, or guides, for flourishing are discrete, nor do we mean to imply that they are independent of each other. Noticing, nurturing, sustaining and flourishing will shift and grow as we attend over and over again to the experience of living from a space of appreciative inquiry, of what makes us feel well, whole, alive, and purposeful in our work and life. We offer these four signals as an organizational tool, and hope that the reader is able to see them as we do—interdependent, iterative, responsive, and dynamic.

As indicated, this book is dedicated to helping teachers flourish and schools become more positive organizations/communities. Built on a critical mass of research, these pages are designed to encourage and coach you to give enhanced attention to **what is working**. As teachers, we know the basic, but crucial, insight connected to the phenomenon that we get more out of what we give attention to. In researching what gives life and what constitutes flourishing, we have focused more on how to develop and sustain thriving communities as part of the work towards our personal fulfillment as teachers. A goal for this book is that the readers will be informed, inspired, and encouraged to learn about and experience the power of the "positive sciences" for their own flourishing as educators - and as individuals. We will spend more time in a later chapter exploring this construct, and how we see it as central to your work as an educator. We will also add our comments and encouragement to informal and formal leaders about ways that teachers may be supported in their pursuit of wellbeing. In the meantime, part of experiencing this learning is tuning into yourself, and we offer a series of reflections and practices that we hope provide opportunity to reflect on who you are as you chart your path toward flourishing.

Toward a Flourishing Pedagogy: Heart Prints and Shifting Ground Moments

Heart Prints are opportunities to reflect on theory and practice in ways that connect you to what matters most to you. We all know about footprints and handprints—these are the impressions that we leave as we pass through the various spaces in our life. Heart Prints is the term that we use for strong emotional impressions that are left on us, and that we leave on others, when we engage from a space of authenticity, wholeness, vulnerability, love, compassion, and so on. These impressions can sometimes inspire us to delve deeper into our own potential for fulfilling our purpose through our work as teachers. **Heart Prints** are opportunities to reflect on our wholeness and to re-connect with our self from a source of deep reflection and inspiration. **Heart Prints** give attention to our personal and professional identity, our passions, our promises, our purposes. We hope that these reflection moments will have lasting impressions on you and your orientation to life, work, and the world. **Heart Print** reflections are opportunities to help us tap into a sense of gratitude and appreciation from the moments when we see our own goodness and our capacities to engage wholeheartedly in life. **Heart Print** stories transcend the boundaries of intellectual or social learning to deeply engage our hearts as we interpret and make sense of our experiences. We invite you to physically feel your **Heart Prints** and experience their transformative power. The **Heart Prints** are your starting point to solicit your true capacity, capabilities, and potentials through a process of reflection, engagement, and transformation.

Helping you develop attention to your stories is one part of a **flourishing pedagogy**, a practice or habit used to enrich or encourage a sense of flourishing in self and others. Through reflection on theories, stories, and practices, **Heart Prints** provide opportunities to pay attention to how we story our work and life, and to notice the new stories that can emerge from a space of deep creativity and inspiration as we tune in to our heart and mind.

The second part of flourishing pedagogy is **Shifting Ground**.

These moments are designed as reflective, creative, and re-creative experiences. The earth is constantly in motion, and all of us who inhabit it are perpetually aware that the ground is always shifting beneath us - both literally and metaphorically. A colleague once commented that "terra firma is no longer so firma." We recall books such as *Stop the World I Want to Get Off*, or Anthony Gidden's *Runaway World*. These remind us of the relentless pace of our lives, and how, as humans and institutions, we have sometimes responded by "hollowing" out our identities and existences. We often resist acknowledging the shifting ground because we might feel more comfortable in our habits and assumptions; the old tapes keep running and the old—even false—narratives, keep playing. Feeling the ground shift beneath our feet can feel scary. We are thrown a bit off kilter, but it's at these times, when we are a little disturbed or placed in dis-ease, that we find spaces for new learning and renewal. These "creative pit stops" are intended to stir up new ideas and shift the ground under you just enough so that you might see new ways of seeing, being, doing. These flourishing pedagogies are intended to serve as provocations for you to reflect on your flourishing.

≋

Noticing **Heart Prints** and nurturing **Shifting Ground** are powerful practices because what we pay attention to will grow. There is a plethora of learning theory that supports this idea: Heliotropic principle (we grow to the light, to the good and to what nourishes), positive action theory, self-determination theory (SDT), the Pygmalion effect, the poietic effect, and so on. If we focus on what is not working (negative deviance), then we more clearly see the multiplied difficulties. Rather, if we focus on what is working, then the positive effects will grow (and even begin to characterize our experiences). We have distilled the theory and practice we have gathered from our research, published work, and our conversations with teachers, into the form of this book. It is intended to be a learning guide, a **Living Map of Flourishing** for you, our reader. We hope that you will engage with us as a way of starting—or continuing—your own inquiry, identifying your own destinations and needed directions, and establishing your own set of gauges as you create your own **Living Map** of what it means for you to flourish in your work.

As you'll see in the next two pages, we've provided an example of our Living Map of Flourishing. This is a snapshot of the theoretical and experiential terrain we will cover through this book—an illustration of the learning experiences that we've pulled together over the course of our research. Part of the beauty of a Living Map is that it will shift and change as you grow and learn; it will reflect your preferences, interests, passions, and purposes, and some of these will change over the course of time as you learn, change, and grow.

This map reflects the findings and learning from our research, offered to you as a possible way into your own learning about wellbeing. We show you the full map of the learning journey that makes up this book here at the outset, to give you some sense of where we are going. You'll notice that there are depictions of the **Heart Print** and **Shifting Ground** moments that will appear throughout the book.

FLOURISHING SCHOOL
REFLECT ON WAYS YOU EXPERIENCE...
FLOURISHING
POWER OF LANGUAGE TO SHAPE OUR STORIES
CREATIVE PIT STOP
COLLAGE
DESIGN YOUR SCHOOL
EMPATHY MEETING
WONDER BY A RIVER
hmm.
CREATE A NEW STORY OF TEACHING
RE-STORY YOUR SCHOOL

SAY YES TO WHAT IS IN FRONT OF ME
WRITE A LEGACY LETTER
CELEBRATION CIRCLE
USE YOUR SENSES
SEND LOVE
MINDFUL MOMENT
QUESTIONS SHIFT FOCUS
WHO AM I AT MY BEST?
DebbieDonsky.com
@DebbieDonsky

We also have designs that represent several of the key ideas that you'll find woven throughout the theory and activities. We hope you find the illustration to be a playful invitation to join with us in exploring the great terrain of flourishing; of course, everyone will eventually make their own maps and chart their own course.

We also wanted to signal with this map that charting, or documenting, our learning is an important part of the process toward wellbeing. As we know from positive psychology, savouring positive experiences can help magnify and extend them (Lyubomirksy, 2006), and so we see this map as a tool you may utilize throughout the various parts of the book so that you may rest with them, savour them, and reap the benefits of lingering with positive emotions and experiences. We also think this map can be of use after you have read the book, and have had a chance to try out the various **Heart Print** and **Shifting Ground** moments.

And with our assertion that this is a lifelong process, we hope that your journey toward wellbeing will include returning to this book in the future. With that intent we also suggest that the map may become a helpful tool for heading with purpose to various parts of the book that you might want to revisit, spend more time with, or share with your colleagues. We have provided the designs for each piece of the map throughout the chapters to help you easily locate particular sections of the book. We hope our map inspires you to be charting your learning and growth in a creative, deeper, more playful, and more engaged way as you create your own Living Map; one that reflects your personality, interests, passions, and playfulness. We hope that your map becomes an enjoyable place for you to contemplate and imagine your way forward in living out your desires for flourishing in your work and life. We encourage you to use the map—and this book—in the way that best works for you. As you'll see in later chapters, we have left some space on the pages for you to jot down ideas that may emerge as read through the activities; we are excited to get started with you as you make your way through this book!

In Chapter Two we describe the current reality for many teachers, the feeling of suffering under the weight of work pressures and demands within environments that do not support their desire for wellbeing. We share some research on stress, exhaustion, and burnout for teachers; what we know is the stark reality that we must face as we suggest a move toward re-orienting our schools for greater attention and focus on flourishing for teachers, students, and all members of the learning community.

In Chapter Three we outline this proposed shift in focusing toward flourishing, and describe our suggestions for how and why we ought to pay attention to the storying process within our schools as an opportunity for new expressions and feelings of flourishing. We offer that re-imagining the work of teaching toward flourishing can happen as we shift our mindsets toward noticing and nurturing wellbeing.

In Chapter Four we provide an overview of *Noticing* flourishing in schools, and offer a possible template for a flourishing inquiry. We also introduce you to the first **Heart Print** and **Shifting Ground** moments. Through these moments we aim to draw attention to opportunities for you to engage in personal reflection and action toward growing wellbeing. In this chapter we also introduce our idea for you to create your own **Living Map**, the ongoing opportunity for you to document your learning journey toward flourishing.

In Chapter Five we provide a brief overview of the research and theory that can be useful for *Nurturing* flourishing through growing knowledge and developing competencies. In this chapter, we introduce the conceptual model of Flourishing in Schools, and describe the research literature that informed our thinking about the domains and professional virtues that synergistically combine in ways to grow flourishing in schools. These theories will give you a more full understanding of the research being carried out in the fields of positive psychology and positive organizational scholarship, as well as research on learning community and living systems theory that influence how we think about organizing schools for flourishing. Throughout this chapter, we encourage you to take time to reflect on your learning, and to capture and document your learning on your **Living Map of Flourishing** developed in the previous chapter.

In Chapter Six we introduce the notion of *sustaining* flourishing through building community. Growing and sustaining wellbeing has often been thought to be the purview of the individual. In this chapter, we outline the imperative of focusing on community as an integral and essential aspect of educator wellbeing. We describe the importance of shared leadership for building community in schools, and highlight the importance of the principal for cultivating and sustaining conditions for flourishing learning communities.

In Chapter Seven we deepen our argument for ensuring wellbeing is a community endeavour. We reiterate the importance of a living-systems view, where individual and community needs are not in competition, but rather are valued as learning opportunities for working together to grow conditions for flourishing for all. In this chapter, we take a reflective look at our learning journey and think about how to carry this work forward into more schools, with more teachers, and across the wider educational community. We offer final reflections and a culminating **Heart Print** and **Shifting Ground** moment to bring together the signals of noticing, nurturing, and sustaining toward the final signal, *flourishing;* the aspirational signal we think is the ultimate goal of living a good life as a teacher.

In Chapter Eight we provide an Epilogue for school leaders. We have sought to honour the vital roles and responsibilities of formal and informal school leaders with respect to teacher wellbeing. We offer some behaviours that we've observed in "way-making" servant leaders who have come alongside teachers. While we know that the messages and ideas contained in the chapter are relevant and meaningful for all teachers, we have sought to encourage and exhort formal and informal school administrators and superintendents to look after their own wellbeing and foster the wellbeing of their teacher colleagues.

We are so pleased that you have found this book, and welcome you to this journey. We hope you find this book to be a companion as you continue or begin (anew) this learning journey. We know that teachers are often relied upon to be the beacons of hope for their students. Teachers are often the ones who shine a light for their students and help them to pay attention to their strengths, their talents, and their passions. Often it is teachers who are the ones to help bring to life a higher version of each student, helping them to see and live out their greatest potentials. We aim for this book to serve as a galvanizer, or animator, of hope and inspiration for you, as the teacher. We share your passion, love and joy of learning, and for fostering hope in others, for being their support and providing encouragement for students to grow, stretch, challenge, and reach for their dreams and desires to work through their challenges, and to live life with purpose. We aim for this book to come alongside you in your role as a hope-bearer, a tool for shining a light on your own strengths, passions, desires, and purposes. We trust you will find comfort and inspiration in this book, and that you will stretch yourself toward noticing, nurturing, and sustaining flourishing in yourself and others.

We offer this book as a starting point for a learning journey of well-being that encourages you, the reader, to practice and explore flourishing through intentionally noticing and nurturing what works well for you to sustain wellbeing in your work and life, and move forward on your journey toward flourishing. We want to encourage those who are already finding healthy ways of flourishing to become even more refreshed and resilient. In the end, our hope is that you will have a custom-built plan, a theory-of-action, that is unique to you but influenced by a process of reflection and a framework of theory and stories, all of which will extend into your own personal sense-making and professional experiences. In reading further, you are engaging with, and becoming part of, our Flourishing Learning Community (FLC). We welcome you, and are so happy to start this journey together.

Chapter Two

Teacher Wellbeing Matters

Teacher wellbeing matters. Period. It matters because teachers are a crucial link to students and their families, and if we want *them* to be well, then we need to attend to the persons who are directly influence and encourage that wellbeing and positive growth—teachers. It matters because teachers deserve to work in conditions that allow for and encourage them to be well. It matters because we are at a crucial time for re-orienting our schools toward providing the kinds of learning, support, and encouragement we need for children to thrive during their time in school—and in their future. The kinds of learning opportunities we want for all our students require teachers who are engaged, collaborative, resilient, innovative, and enthused about the ongoing professional learning required, and this requires attention to their thriving so that they may pursue their teaching from a sense of purpose, and with passion, zest, and vitality.

As we have said, teachers are vital links to supporting and growing the kinds of communities we all want to live in and leave for future generations, and so it makes ethical and moral sense that we should all be interested in caring for those who care for our children. For us, what it comes down to is that teachers, just like all persons in all kinds of work, need and deserve environments that will support them in ensuring they can attend to self-care so that they may thrive in their work. Our own interest in wellbeing developed over several years, especially as we began to notice it seemed to be missing in the extant research on school improvement. We believe there is a moral and ethical imperative for supporting the wellbeing of teachers. Our logic was that if school improvement is fundamentally about teachers thinking and acting in healthy ways that meaningfully improve learning and loving in schools, then the heart of school improvement is dependent on the wellbeing of those teachers and their capacity to lead learning with moral purpose (Sergiovanni, 1996; Marzano, Waters & McNulty, 2005).

With those teachers and principals we have engaged in our ongoing research, we've learned more about how they develop and maintain professional learning communities (PLCs) (Cherkowski, 2012, 2016; Cherkowski & Schnellert, 2016, 2017; Sackney & Walker, 2007; Sackney, Walker & Mitchell, 2005), and we recognized that the school improvement research was missing a holistic perspective. PLCs can provide much sustenance for teachers and administrators to join together in the work toward school improvement. However, we wondered why there was little mention about the passion, inspiration, and joy—as well as the suffering, anguish and disappointments—that we know exist in the realities of teachers' work lives. Conversations at all levels of the system seemed to avoid these elements, and as we looked at both the research regarding, and practice of, school improvement, such as expressed in the widely recognized PLC model, the silence was deafening.

We began to talk with each other, and to explore in the literature, stories, and ideas, about what it might mean to experience our work as a fully human endeavour; an endeavour where those in educational environments honour, embrace, and build on both the sufferings and the joys of work in schools. As we will share with you in later chapters, we began to explore with an ear to positive psychology, positive organizational scholarship, and appreciative approaches that engage in human dynamics and change. Within these fields, we found insights and practices for seeing the work of school improvement from humanistic, appreciative, and holistic perspectives.

As we grew our own knowledge of the positive sciences, we opened our hearts and minds to what it might mean to re-imagine schools from positive, generative, appreciative, and humanistic insights. During these imaginings and reflections, our main research question emerged. This question has been at the heart of our research, and each time we revisit our thinking on teacher wellbeing and flourishing this question propels us forward to new ways of exploring and imagining the beauty and awe entailed in flourishing schools:

What if you were to imagine that your primary role as an educator is to learn how to thrive in your role, and, in so doing, to continually co-explore and to enthusiastically facilitate all means by which each person in your learning community flourishes along with you, most of the time?

As indicated, we continue to see ourselves primarily as teachers, even in our roles as university academics. We cherish the opportunities to connect and learn along with teachers, mainly through our research activities, through our teacher education opportunities, and through our engagement with educational leaders. Given our affinity with teaching, as a profession and a calling, we feel aligned with this posed question and believe that it is just the right question of our time, especially as many among us struggle to make sense of this profession and the strenuous demands placed upon the school as workplace.

It was Jack Miller (2007) who suggested, "education, specifically, has done much to sever the relationship between head and heart. Anything that is not part of academic discourse is labeled 'touchy-feely.' As a result, in industrialized society, we live in our heads, denying our deeper knowing and intuitions" (p. 4). Much longer ago, Blaise Pascal, the famous French scientist and philosopher, was attributed with having said, "the heart has its reasons of which reason knows nothing." Far too often, teachers experience their work as fragmented rather than whole; they are pushed to account for merely the cognitive achievements of their students, leaving aside the many social, emotional, and spiritual aspects of learning and development that are essential to students' wellbeing. More often than not, these capacities are also what provides the sustenance for teachers' careers, as they foster and deepen relationships with students and colleagues through developing the social and emotional aspects of learning and education. There is certainly a growing shift toward providing a more holistic approach to schooling that takes into account the importance of social and emotional development. However, we know that Miller's assertion that these competencies, and the activities designed to develop them, are often deemed by skeptics as "touchy-feely" or soft. As a consequence, these same life-giving elements are left to the margins in what is often an already over-full student curriculum or teacher support system.

Increasingly, in our rapidly shifting, volatile, and uncertain educational landscapes, teachers are called upon to engage as learning leaders in well-intentioned initiatives that are generally aimed at increasing educational outcomes and ensuring equity across the school. These can be laudable aims. Teachers often take on leadership roles outside of their classrooms to contribute to these efforts. While these opportunities provide moments for both personal and professional impact, learning, and growth, there can also be engagement moments that present themselves with feelings of being overtaxed and overwhelmed. These are the moments that run counter to increased teacher wellbeing. Heroically—and typically alone—teachers try to handle the increasingly complex and challenging work of classroom education and school improvement through various processes.

Stress, Burnout, and Costs to the Education System

Increased stress and resulting mental health concerns are contemporary issues in workplaces worldwide. These concerns are influenced by decisions made from various levels of government and have resulted in stunning costs to the economy and to health care systems (Naylor, 2008). From the economic perspective, psychological distress, an indicator of poor mental health, strains organizations in many ways, including increased costs associated with higher employee absences, greater long-term disability pensions, and accelerated retirements resulting from mental illness (Leijon, Balliu, Lundin & Hemmingsson, 2017). Of course, the cost of stress also impacts individual employees (Naylor, 2008). As a Swedish study on the general working population demonstrated, employees who reported psychological distress (unhappiness accompanied by feelings of anxiety and depression) had a higher likelihood of evaluating themselves as having poor work ability (Leijon et al., 2017). Rates of job dissatisfaction and psychological distress were also demonstrated to independently influence subsequent work absences in a sample of health service providers (Hardy, Woods & Wall, 2003). It is imperative that organizations prioritize the implementation of strategies to decrease employee psychological distress as a means to achieve organizational sustainability (Leijon et al., 2017).

Employees in the health, social service, and education industries suffer a significant risk of experiencing compassion fatigue due to the taxing nature of emotional demands and empathic engagement. Simply doing an internet search on stress in the helping professions will bring up websites of associations and unions all over the world who are dedicated to helping their members recognize, and recover from, stress, exhaustion, and burnout. These conditions can and often do advance to produce the damaging experiences of vicarious traumatization and burnout (Naylor, 2008). It is not hard to fathom that the profession of teaching generates similarly unfriendly conditions; especially when we consider that many teachers spend upwards of 700 hours a year with their students, excluding additional daily duties such as preparing lessons, marking, performing general administrative tasks, attending professional development seminars and staff meetings, collaborating with other teachers, meeting with community members or parents, supervising students at recesses, counselling, and taking on a variety of other extra or co-curricular tasks. Many of these additional activities are voluntary and discretionary manifestations of teacher diligence and good will in the service of students and their families (OECD, 2016). In addition, teachers spend much of their teaching time managing the increased complexities of their 21st Century classrooms. These contexts can add yet another layer of stressful circumstances to teachers trying to negotiate the myriad special needs and attentions required by their students. Adding these dimensions to the typical classroom management of student misbehaviours means that teachers are engaged in significant disciplinary and management actions while ensuring the wide-range of student learning is progressing well (Fernet et al., 2012). The four main sources of stress for teachers include the school's environment (comprised of school administration and school culture), job demands, the resources and support available for teachers to make their own decisions, and teachers' personal level of social-emotional competency (Greenberg et al., 2016). It is easy to comprehend the often times taxing environments in which teachers carry out their work.

Consequently, chronic stress at work will often lead to burnout (Bermejo-Toro et al., 2016). This research highlights that burnt out teachers experience negative consequences in their overall health, job performance, and relationships with colleagues, family, and friends. Burnout can be better understood as a process where emotional exhaustion leads to symptoms of cognitive stress and impairments in teacher's daily tasks, which then result in burnout (Feuerhahn, Stamov-RoBnagel, Wolfram, Bellingrath, & Kudielka, 2013). Additionally, teachers' experience of burnout symptoms can fluctuate throughout the academic year and are influenced by their perceptions of their work environment, as well as their level of autonomous motivation and self-efficacy (Fernet et al., 2012).

A Gallup poll (data tracked from Jan. 3, 2013 to Sept. 30, 2014) indicated that approximately 70% of US teachers are either not engaged in their work (lacking effort and an emotional connection to their job) or actively disengaged in their work (expressing their unhappiness in a way that impacts coworkers) (Hastings & Agrawal, 2015). It is projected that this group will miss 2.3 million more workdays, over their career spans, than teachers who are engaged in their work (Hastings & Agrawal, 2015). Absenteeism costs school systems time and money; they need to find and pay substitute teachers, which then also disrupts lesson plans and creates inconsistent classroom environments for student learning and their continuity of care (Greenberg et al., 2016; Hastings & Agrawal, 2015). Unfortunately a large numbers of teachers leave the profession due to the types of circumstances mentioned above (Kutsyuruba & Walker, 2017). For example, a recent-issue brief by Pennsylvania State University reported that between 23% and 42% of teachers leave the profession, often within the first five years, impacting student achievement. The impact is particularly felt by low performing students and costs schools between $4,000 and $17,000 for every teacher who leaves the profession (Greenberg et al., 2016).

There are challenges that come to us that we are capable of dealing with, and then there are challenges we encounter that are beyond us and out of our control. For example, the education system is changing, as a large proportion of teachers will retire within the next decade. Given that the proportion of the school-aged population will increase, there is an impending high demand for teachers worldwide (OECD, 2016). Financial constraints, such as pension obligations and health-care costs, for teachers who have retired, will increase the pressures on governments to make changes to the education system; this may include decreasing academic offerings, raising the number of students per classroom, and adding more online, self-directed learning programs (OECD, 2016). These conditions and pressures, combined with the incessant, and often unrealistic, ongoing demands for increased student performance, will mean that high-quality teachers may leave the profession from lack of support, frustration, and/or from the experience of discouraging work environments (OECD, 2016). These demands continue to be part of the generative and adaptive conversations that engage politicians, public bureaucrats, and local policy makers about schooling and education. Despite the obvious relevance of these conditions, the conversations, decisions, policy and support structures are often beyond the control of the teacher, or even groups of teachers.

For teachers, burnout tends to refer to a syndrome of emotional exhaustion, depersonalization – a negative, cynical attitude towards one's work—and a reduced sense of personal accomplishment (Skaalvik & Skaalvik, 2007). Basically, burnout can be easily described as feeling worn out or empty (Carmona, Buunk, Peiro, Rodrigues & Bravo, 2006) or "out of gas." As we described, some main causes of burnout include unwieldy time pressures, threats to one's personal or professional identity, feeling judged about one's performance in a personalized way, feeling powerless, and a general feeling of not doing an important enough and meaningful job (Carmona et al., 2006; Froeschle & Crews, 2010; Skaalvik & Skaalvik, 2007, 2009).

When the larger social or school system is pushed towards meeting multiple short-term markers of achievements, for the sake of outside or external demands, then those who bear the pressures (teachers within that system) may experience burnout or feel they are being exploited by de-personalized, unrelenting, and oppressive top-down systems of bureaucracy (Hargreaves & Fullan, 2012). Given the complexity, pressures, and demands of this work, it is not surprising that highly dedicated teachers who work tirelessy to meet the needs of their students will experience emotional and physical exhaustion. This can be brought about by frustration, anxiety, and uncertainty about whether or not they feel they will be able to perform to what can feel like unrealistic and impossible expectations (Skaavik & Skaalvik, 2007). We might think "people are counting on me; but perhaps they don't understand I am only one person and the work is much more complex than meets the eye!" One can succumb, often incrementally, to emotional exhaustion over a period of time (Skaalvik & Skaalvik, 2009).

Of course this thinking and exhaustive conditions are detrimental to our natural personal needs for wellbeing. As we have, perhaps you too have met teachers who have ended up feeling bitter and resentful of their work; they have confided their feelings that teaching has taken up all or too much of their life energy and has "sucked them dry." Other teachers have emotionally given up, but keep going in to their work as a daily, tired obligation. There is an old saying that "as the weight of the cart increased, the ox bowed its head to the ground." Perhaps you've occasionally sighted such a person with their head pulled down or a mask on to hide their distress; you might have even seen this person in the mirror from time to time. We all have a propensity to create an artificial persona, or mask, to hide our distress and defend ourselves in times of modest-to-severe vulnerability. We think there are ways forward that are within our control that can help us to notice when we are putting on these masks, bowing our heads to the ground from the weight of our work and life, and generally heading toward the path of burnout. At these times, some relief may come from noticing where we do have a sense of ownership in our work, and to then nurture moments of efficacy and autonomy in our own learning, growth, and development (Kegan & Wagner, 2013).

Toward Wellbeing: Re-imagining a New Way Forward

We fully support the ongoing work of those in positions of power to ensure that teachers are part of the conversations for changes that will affect what happens in schools; we also think it is important for teachers to reflect on what is within the range of their own choosing. A sense of wellbeing includes focusing on that which is within our power to amend, moderate, or navigate. When teachers clearly identify, within what is desired or hoped for, that which they themselves can do without encumbrance or permission, then some of the frustration, anxiety, and agitation can be alleviated. Much—albeit not all—of one's personal health and response to workplace change can be ordered by personal choice.

So, what if we were to shift our mindsets to think about the work of teaching as including a strong sense of wholeness and aliveness? As we mentioned earlier, mindsets are core beliefs that serve as filters for how we see the world, and that reflect our philosophies of life (McGonigal, 2015). Along with mindset researchers (Dweck, 2006; McGonigal, 2015), we suggest that we can learn to shift our mindsets to more aptly reflect our desires for wellbeing, even in stressful work such as teaching. What if we were to interrogate our mindsets about teaching? What if we noticed, and let sink in, new ways of talking about teaching, such as "good teaching requires self-cultivation rather than self-sacrifice" (Higgins, 2011, p. 131)? Don't get us wrong here. We get self-sacrifice (in its best sense of compassionate service to others); but as we all know, you can't serve others from an empty self or feed other people from an empty shelf. It may be just semantics, but we think selfless service is the last thing we need. In ideal terms, what we need is whole-self service to others that is, from time to time, self-sacrificing or altruistic. We know from experience that most teachers are givers rather than takers, so it is essential that we create new ways of thinking and talking about this delicate balance of teachers giving and taking in their work.

As teachers ourselves, we have struggled with moments of feeling overwhelmed and feeling inadequate in our various roles in our own work. On reflection, we have noticed that at these times we are often not working from our strengths. The metaphors of juggling, plate spinning, burning the candle at both ends, running on fumes, and working off the corner of our desks are all too familiar. We recall times of feeling unwell as we've wrestled with how to "survive," "hold our breath," or "suffer through" the heaped-up pile of responsibilities and seemingly undiminishing piles of tasks and accumulated items on our checklists. Learning from our journey, we have come to understand what it means to experience more and more wellbeing in our work.

Of course, learning to live the disciplines of boundary-setting, creating margins, or white space, and realizing that every "yes" is a "no" to a future opportunity have been helpful. However, we've noticed that the questions we have begun to ask about how to shift the ways we think about school improvement toward a more holistic, appreciative, and positive perspective have created shifts for us in our thinking. As we asked our questions, we started to notice how some schools and colleague-teachers flourish in their work, and we started to open new spaces within our thinking to explore school improvement and the demands of 21st Century education. This newly created question-space invited us to uncover what happens when we work and live from a strength-based perspective. We noticed where the saying, "an educator-fanatic is someone who, having lost their sense of direction, simply doubles their speed," might be lived out more often that it should be in our own workplaces, and in the work of our teacher-colleagues in other educational contexts.

As we continued to explore the possibilities that can emerge when we frame teaching, relating, leading, and working from a place of passion, purpose, strengths, and vitality, we wondered about these same possibilities in terms of the organizational structures and systems of schools. When we have thought about organizing schools from appreciative, positive, holistic, strengths-based, life-giving perspectives we know that we are moving down a new path, a new way of thinking about the work of teaching, learning, and leading schools. As we join with you now, to chart together a path of wellbeing for teachers, we want to spend some time describing what it might mean to flourish in schools. This is a state of being that will look very different among and between teachers, and among and between schools.

Chapter Three

Shifting Mindsets Toward Flourishing

We believe that wellbeing at work for teachers means moving beyond an expectation of merely surviving the challenges and hardships that this work can bring. Wellbeing at work means finding ways to thrive, feeling a sense of vitality and zest at work, all the while growing and filling out individual and collective potentials throughout one's teaching career. We propose that a shift in mindset toward viewing the work of teaching as learning to flourish, so that we can model and encourage others to shift toward this mindset in their own work and life, is an essential aspect of moving toward wellbeing for teachers. We think a mindset shift toward flourishing provides new openings, or spaces, for imagining the work of teaching in ways that promote what makes us feel well, whole, and alive in our work. We propose that an agentic stance of wellbeing—noticing and then claiming the spaces in our lives that are within our control for shifting our responses and actions to promote and encourage wellbeing for self and others—is an opportunity for a mindset shift toward flourishing.

But, the challenge in accomplishing this is significant: we are concerned that teachers' levels of wellbeing are overestimated. In most countries of the world, mental health is by far the most serious and most pervasive of human unwellness. There is a prevalence of thinking that if "it" isn't an obvious issue, then "it" isn't an issue; there is also the equally problematic view that "you are either mentally ill or you are not." We assume that our wellbeing includes our mental, physical, emotional, and spiritual aspects, and that all of us live on continua of wellbeing in the various dimensions of our lives. In studies across numerous nations, workplaces are the leading source of stress and unwellness. There is no clear line between being healthy and being ill; just as there is no clear line between being trustworthy versus unreliable or safe versus dangerous or capable versus incapable or competent versus incompetent.

The mental health continuum model (Figure 2.1) was first conceived by the United States military to normalize mental health fluctuations, to provide some direction and expectation for recovery, and to offer some ways for colleagues and workers to recognize the signs and symptoms of thriving, struggling, or languishing. In this book we have focused on both imagining and experiencing what healthy, happy, and wellbeing looks like, and we suggest that proactive self-care is critical to each teacher's disciplines and practices for their own wellbeing.

HEALTHY	REACTING	INJURED	ILL
✓ Normal mood fluctuations ✓ Calm & takes things in stride ✓ Good sense of humour ✓ Performing well ✓ In control mentally ✓ Normal sleep patterns ✓ Few sleep difficulties ✓ Physically well ✓ Good energy level ✓ Physically & socially active ✓ No or limited alcohol use/ gambling	✓ Irritable/impatient ✓ Nervous ✓ Sadness/ overwhelmed ✓ Displaced sarcasm ✓ Procrastination ✓ Forgetfulness ✓ Trouble sleeping ✓ Intrusive thoughts ✓ Nightmares ✓ Muscle tension/ headaches ✓ Low energy ✓ Decreased activity/ socializing ✓ Regular but controlled alcohol use/gambling	✓ Anger ✓ Anxiety ✓ Pervasively sad/ hopeless ✓ Negative attitude ✓ Poor performance/ workaholic ✓ Poor concentration/ decisions ✓ Restless disturbed sleep ✓ Recurrent images/ nightmares ✓ Increased aches & pains ✓ Increased fatigue ✓ Avoidance ✓ Withdrawal ✓ Increased alcohol use/gambling is hard to control	✓ Angry outbursts/ aggression ✓ Excessive anxiety/ panic attacks ✓ Depressed/suicidal thoughts ✓ Over insubordination ✓ Can't perform duties, control behaviour or concentrate ✓ Can't fall asleep or stay asleep ✓ Sleeping too much or too little ✓ Physical illnesses ✓ Constant fatigue ✓ Not going out or answering phone ✓ Alcohol or gambling addiction ✓ Other addictions

Self-care & Social Support — **Professional Care**

Figure 3.1 Mental Health Continuum Model

Thinking about the continuum model of mental health, there is much to gain by inquiring into the aspect of the continuum in the healthy range that is assumed, but not overtly described—what does it mean to live our teaching life beyond normal functioning, to flourish as a healthy teacher? This question is at the heart of this book, and we hope the question inspires you to put healthfulness at the heart of your own inquiry: How might you live out your work-life in ways that promote your own flourishing and encourage others to do the same?

While we don't want to spend too much time dwelling in spaces of emotional or mental depletion and deficit-thinking, it is helpful to recognize and understand what flourishing is not. And it is important to recognize that we are all at different points in our lives. We also think it is important to note that we are talking about flourishing as an aspiration worthy of striving for, wherever we may be on the continuum. However, for too many teachers their organizational and professional experiences are taking a toll, and this has large costs to them, to their students, to schools, and to society. There are certainly courses and programs available for teachers to learn how to regulate and manage their emotions and reactions to stress. We fully endorse and support these resources, and hope that many teachers are able to access and use these programs to develop structures and strategies to allow them to stay in (or to return to) their work. Our aim is to offer new perspectives, research insights, reflection moments, and activities for growing a sense of flourishing wherever we can in our work through noticing what works well, makes us feel alive, whole, engaged, and connected, and paying attention to ways we can grow more of that in our work. This is not about denying struggles and suffering, because we know these are always part of human experiences. Rather, it is about putting a more intentional focus on wellbeing as an essential aspect of your work as a teacher, and then paying specific attention to how you frame your work to promote and encourage self-care, positive growth and development, and a sense of thriving for self and others in your particular context. Knowing the potential of language as a structuring force in our social experiences (Gergen, 2009), and as an opportunity for transforming our thoughts and actions (Dweck, 2010; McGonigal, 2015), we think there is much to be gained from supporting teachers in learning how to frame their work in ways that enlivens and emboldens their agentic stance of wellbeing.

Storying Self-care as Essential and Valuable Work

What if the assumption underpinning our profession boldly asserted that a necessary condition for being effective was for every educator to *first* give attention to their on-going self-cultivation? Throughout this book, we encourage you to pay attention to the stories you tell yourself about what it means to be an educator, and to notice how those stories are serving your personal and professional wellbeing. What are the dominant narratives in your teacher-life? Are all your stories true, or are there some false narratives in your repertoire? While you may not be able to radically alter the challenging working conditions that seem to inhibit your personal and professional growth, or substantially change what often feels like a negative public opinion of the role of the educator, you may be able to reframe the stories that you tell (to yourself and others) about who you are and what your work is. In reality, we can't always have what we believe to be the best conditions or circumstances, but we do have some domains of choice. For a moment, assume with us that through this re-storying process you can find new pathways towards attaining your own sense of thriving in your work as a teacher-educator.

How Stories Shape our Realities

What do you see, hear, and feel when you read our overarching inquiry question:

> **What if you imagine that your primary role as a teacher is to learn how to thrive in your role, and, in so doing, continually co-explore and enthusiastically facilitate all means by which everyone in your learning communities flourishes, most of the time?**

Do you feel a deep desire to thrive and grow? Do you experience a physical or visceral response to the term 'flourish?' What do you feel as you think about cultivating a community where everyone is flourishing, or on their way to doing so? For us, and the teachers we have worked with, contemplating 'flourishing' is a way to begin to notice and articulate how, when and why we feel a sense of thriving in our work. Not surprisingly, when asked this question, teachers described that they felt a sense of flourishing when their students thrive. They get a deep sense of meaning and joy from connecting with and seeing the positive differences they are making in their students' lives. They also shared that enjoying a high level of wellbeing in their work was connected to experiences of support, care, and collegial engagement. They felt a sense of flourishing when they had fun and laugh often at work, when they taught from their passion and when they experienced meaning and purpose.

Teachers are faced with real pressures and challenges as they learn to teach in new ways in schools. Pedagogical redesign that encourages the kinds of teaching and learning necessary to prepare 21st Century young people can be challenging. Given the increased international attention to preparing students differently than we have in the past, for a future characterised by increasing uncertainty, rapid change, and more complexity, we understand that this pressure for new learning can seem overwhelming and daunting for teachers. We understand that often times there has been insufficient support provided for teachers—mental, emotional, pedagogical, organizational, and we could go on. With you, we appreciate that this rapidly-changing educational landscape can seem fraught with risk-taking, uncertainty, and fear. This is a very real interpretation of what it can feel like for teachers faced with preparing their students for the uncertainty and complexity of the 21st Century. And yes, this is just the tip of the iceberg. We haven't even mentioned our living with domestic demands and interacting with family, extended family, friends, and community members, as well as the demands and pressures of aiming to be contributing citizens in our increasingly interconnected, diverse, and globalized society.

Given all of this, we suggest that this is an opportunity to orient teachers and schools towards wellbeing, and towards a focus on a holistic perspective on schooling; an encouragement to develop the minds, bodies, and spirits of teachers and their students. We know that teachers want and need practices and strategies for attaining and growing their wellbeing, and so we offer this tool/book for teachers, individuals, teams, and schools and districts. We offer a starting point for anyone interested in focusing on wellbeing as a central tenet in what it means to be a teacher. For some, reading this may be coming at a time when they are on the verge of giving up their hope of finding a sense of wellbeing, of purpose, and of passion in their work. They are understandably suffering from years of trying to do their best work with their students, but not having had the supports and encouragement to value and maintain their wellbeing as a primary focus of their work. They might tell us they feel exhausted, burnt out, and disappointed that the hopes they had for their work and the pleasures of teaching now seem impossible undertakings. There is also despair, as they have ground away at the seemingly endless lists of outcomes, tasks, responsibilities, and jobs that take them further and further away from what they most care about—their students and the learning they'd hoped to engender in this up and coming generation.

Storying Schools as Thriving Living Systems

We think it is time to honour and value wellbeing for our teachers so that we can grow and build flourishing in all our schools, for all our learning community members. The stories we share—and encourage you to develop—are rooted in flourishing professional community, developed through positive and appreciative perspectives. In the last number of years, we have seen how talk about schooling has lost the heart and soul of teaching and learning, and forgotten about the importance of cultivating schools as living systems of people working together toward a deeper and stronger humanity. We think schools can be places for individuals and groups to work together toward bettering humanity. However, we have posited that much of the talk about schooling tends to be deficit-oriented and cynical with inferences of blame and shame for under-performance. These narratives reflect and perpetuate a belief that schools are systems to be managed, with the people within them as objects to be kept under control. If we want to transform our schools to achieve their potential as vehicles for bettering humanity, we need to shift our stories to be able to see schools in new ways (Cherkowski & Walker, 2013).

We see schools as living systems, characterized by notions of interconnection, diversity, interdependence, emergence and renewal (Capra, 2004; Senge, 2006; Scharmer, 2009). From this ecological metaphor, we can see schools as a complex web of relationships within which we carry out our work; diverse groups of people joining together in interconnected and interdependent ways in the pursuit of an ever-deepening, personal and collective fulfillment of their humanity. Adding to this metaphor, the idea of flourishing means that we see schools as life-giving systems, vital and energizing. We know this is a different way to think and talk about schools. We share this because we know that this shift in language and imagination can make a difference in how we work towards what we ultimately desire—spaces and places where vibrant, engaged, passionate, caring, and meaningful experiences happen for us all as we focus on our core work: teaching and learning. We suggest that as teachers shift their stories about teaching toward one of flourishing in living systems, they can develop their living theories and life-giving practices to intentionally create communities where their students (including their families) and colleagues (teachers, administrators) can thrive.

Heart Print

Shifting the view of teacher professional learning and development as a commitment to ongoing development of, and reflection on, living theories and life-giving practices places a greater priority on the importance of self-cultivation through teaching, rather than considering the view of teaching as an isolating and selfless act that happens only for the good of the student (Higgins, 2011). Higgins argued that teachers can model self-cultivation and self-care as an essential element of education. In doing so their students are able to engage in their own self-cultivation and self-care. We'd like to suggest that it is possible for teachers to lie to themselves or to incrementally adopt scripts or inner narratives that are patently false and unhelpful. We wonder if you will relate to a fictional scenario that depicts a progression; one beginning with idealism, followed by burnout and, finally, ending with a stifling, negative presence of an educator:

1. I recognize that teaching is a deeply moral task. Foremost in my mind I strive to remember that my chief concern is my students, their needs, and their development;
2. But when I do this job well, thinking only of their welfare, I am not able to give as much of myself to satisfying my own desires to have rich and stimulating experiences, to keep growing and changing. In trying to live up to this moral ideal I find that I demand an endless giving of myself, which leaves me spent and exhausted;
3. There is not enough time outside of work to rejuvenate myself, but it is one of the worst betrayals of teaching to try to meet my own needs through my students; I will have to content myself with the fact that one must personally sacrifice in order to do good;
4. The more I accomplish for others, the more I have to sacrifice;
5. The more I sacrifice, the more I must be accomplishing for others;
6. I am a dried-up shell of a person; therefore, I must be a good educator. I'm certainly not here for me, so I must be here for them; and

7. My students should be grateful, but they are so selfish and self-centered. I'll teach them a thing or two. (p. 159)

After reading this passage once, go back and read it a second time. This time feel it, and notice what in the passage resonates within you and your own experiences. Jot down your images, thoughts, and gestures. Try to do this without judgment or self-criticism or blame. Do you connect with this internal dialogue or narrative? Is this script familiar? When you feel ready, can you create a new story of teaching, one that reflects your ideas about the importance of self-cultivation in teaching? How does your story lead to flourishing? Take some time to reflect on how your stories about teaching are lived out in the way you experience your work and vice-versa.

We think schools can be places for individuals and groups to work together toward bettering humanity. However, we have posited that much of the talk about schooling tends to be deficit-oriented and cynical with inferences of blame and shame for under-performance. These narratives reflect and perpetuate a belief that schools are systems to be managed, with the people within them as objects to be kept under control. If we want to transform our schools to achieve their potential as vehicles for bettering humanity, we need to shift our stories to be able to see schools in new ways (Cherkowski & Walker, 2013). Healthy professional autonomy is necessary to be able to address the complex and changing needs of students and to have the competence and confidence to respond to situations immediately (Skaalvik & Skaalvik, 2009). In addition, on-going support from the educational community and positive relations with colleagues increases job satisfaction and decreases stress. Teachers have a collective responsibility to their students, colleagues, and the public, to flourish, even under the current educational conditions (workload, time pressures, lack of support). We understand the pressures and constraints that teachers experience in their work as they strive toward greater professional autonomy. We also suggest that, within the larger political and organizational work of school improvement, teachers can learn to develop their own stance of agency for their wellbeing, and can make choices from within their realm of control to experience levels of personal, ongoing development and autonomy—important aspects of wellbeing and personal growth (Deci & Ryan, 2012; Kegan & Wagner, 2013).

Creating your Living Map

Framing our work as teachers as a pursuit of wellbeing for self and others means designing our work in ways that promote and encourage what makes us feel alive, whole, connected, engaged, and purposeful—among many other descriptors for what it means to feel a sense of thriving. Recently, we have seen how maker-movements have taken hold in schools, with an emphasis on designing, creating, and playing as innovative learning experiences. We have noticed the threads of play, fun, laughter, creativity, and innovation in how teachers describe stories about what makes them come alive, feel engaged, feel connected, have fun and tinker in their work to grow their teaching practices and respond in new ways with their colleagues to the ever-changing dynamics of their classrooms. Interestingly, Daniel Pink (2005) wrote about the growing importance in what he called our "conceptual age" of stimulating, engaging, and learning from our whole brain—using the left (logical, rational) and the right (creative, intuitive) sides of our brain. Pink argued that there has been a long tradition in the Western world to value and prioritise activities that happen in the left brain; activities that are associated with language, sequential reasoning and analysis (p. 14). Activities that seemed connected with the right side (emotional expression and understanding, intuition, imagining, and noticing patterns) had largely been determined to be soft, whimsical, and not as useful for the world we live in. However, with increased understanding of the brain, scientists started to notice how both sides of the brain contributed to important activities. There is a real advantage to using both sides of the brain to access a broader range of intellectual, emotional and health benefits (p. 14). In Pink's (2005) words, those people who are able to tap into and use their right-brain abilities will "rule the future." He described how the right-brain abilities—design, story, symphony, empathy, play, meaning—are those needed in our conceptual age; people who can bring together disparate ideas in ways that are integrative and make sense, or design new spaces and places that can engage communities in deeper meaning in their work, or who can learn how to experience the health and social benefits of play at work, during what can feel like stressful, rushed lives.

While we are not suggesting that teachers who use the right side of their brain will rule the school, we do think that we can begin to use activities that engage and develop our creative, intuitive, emotional talents to build and grow a more full sense of who we are and who we can become as educators. We also see the benefits of using creative activities to tap into and stimulate our thinking from the right side of the brain as we work to develop an understanding of what it means to thrive in our work, and to experience the physical health benefits that are beginning to be associated with creative activities.

In the next section, we provide an overview of several creative activities we have used with teachers to engage them in thinking about and expressing their sense of what it can mean to flourish at work through a creative activity. In this first **Shifting Ground** moment, we invite you to think of ways you might begin to create your **Living Map of Flourishing** template in such a way that you are drawn to use it as a reflecting tool for documenting your learning. This **Living Map** can be an artistic representation of your learning, engaging art to create something with your heart, mind, and hands.

We know that many of you might balk or cringe at the idea of tapping into art to access new learning moments, having decided many years ago that you are not creative, or not the artistic type. We want to assure you that we counted ourselves among that group of "not very creative" people. But, when we changed the stories that we told ourselves about what it means to be creative, we were able to access a new way of experiencing creativity that was more relaxing, enriching, and fun. For example, David Hansen (2005) is an educational philosopher who proposed "that we consider the idea that creativity in teaching often manifests itself most vividly, if also subtly, in a kind of ongoing attentiveness, by which I mean a dynamic combination of patience, listening and initiative" (p. 57). Taking this new perspective on creativity freed us from thinking that we needed to have certain talents or skills to be creative, and guided us to thinking about how to engage with patience, to listen deeply to ourselves and to others, and then to initiate action from that new place of learning. For us, this meant that every learning opportunity was a chance to be creative, to engage with presence and openness to let new ways of thinking and learning emerge. In his model of social learning for deep change, Scharmer (2009) described the importance of developing practices to access a deeper source of learning within, where creativity is always available and endless. He argued that through opening our hearts, minds, and will to the possibility of entering a social field of awareness, through what he calls the "U of learning," groups and individuals can engage in deep learning and creation that allows them to co-create their desired future.

While we are not suggesting that you can only access creativity from a deep-dive learning experience such as that offered through the U of learning, we do suggest that creativity is available to all of us when we are courageous enough to open ourselves to learning from all of our senses and experiences. From this perspective, we suggest that constructing your **Living Map** can be a creative process, and that as you get still, present, and open to learning, and then express your learning from an open mind, open heart, and open will, you might find that you can be creative in surprising ways. The following ideas come from working with teachers through our flourishing in schools research. They used these creative activities to make their maps, and we have found that these were significant products for them, both in the process of making them, and in using them as a reflective tool for their own learning. Each of the ideas might serve as a starting point for your map, or you might find that you connect with both of them and they both make their way into your mapmaking endeavour. As we will continue to say throughout the book, there is no correct way to

engage in learning about your wellbeing—all entry points are worthwhile exploring.

Shifting Ground Creative Idea: Collage

For this first **Shifting Ground**, gather together a good selection of magazines (that you feel okay about cutting up), some glue or tape, and a big piece of poster paper. You are going to start visually representing your **Living Map**. Over time, as you come to enjoy the process of tuning in to your self and playing with a variety of ways of charting your learning, you might find that these "creative pit stops" become a treasured part of your teaching routine.

Figure 3.2 Kelly Hanson's Burning Burnout *Collage*

On a separate piece of paper, make a list of all the things that are fueling what you perceive as burnout, anger, anxiety, or frustration in your work. As you look through magazines, cut out pictures, words, colours, and images that represent those things for you. On your poster paper, use the magazine clippings and some glue or tape to "collage" a destination that represents burnout for you. Notice how you feel as you pay attention to these thoughts and feelings.

Now, make a list of all the thoughts and feelings you associate with a beautiful day, week, or month of teaching. What is your dream image of teaching? How would that dream feel and look like? As you look through magazines, cut out pictures, words, colours, and images that represent those things for you. Use these magazine clippings and some glue or tape to "collage" a destination that represents flourishing for you.

You may also find that creating a digital collage is appealing to you. Our graduate research assistant, Kelly Hanson, developed a beautiful digital collage that represents her **Living Map** (she called it Burning Burnout). Using digital images she created one side of her map to represent when she feels close to burnout in her work. The other side of the map has images of when she feels the most engaged, alive, connected, and encouraged in her work. She has four words threaded throughout the map (connect, contemplate, create, community) that guide her as signposts along the path toward her preferred state of wellbeing (Figure 3.2).

Shifting Ground Creative Idea: Design your School (or home, or club etc.) as Energy Zones

On a large piece of paper, draw a map of your school in as much detail as you can in terms of spaces and places. Once you have finished the map, take a mental tour around your school. Try to feel yourself in the rooms as you visit them in your mind's eye, and jot down images or symbols to represent the kind of energy you feel when you are in these rooms with the people who generally work in them. Do you feel positive or negative energy? Is it encouraging your own energy or does it feel draining? Is it light and playful, or heavy and dull? Take some time to draw your school using symbols and/or images. When you are done, do some reflecting on where you see what Kim Cameron (2008) calls the Energizers; people who tend to build up positive energy in such a way that it influences and infuses others in a positive and generative way. You come away from that room feeling more energy.

On the flip side are those people, spaces, and places that tend to deplete your energy, drag you down. Now that you're warmed up and noticing energy in your school, go to your own classroom and reflect on your own energy, both in your room and throughout the school. Where do you notice you have the most energy? What is contributing to that energy (people, activities, rhythms, routines, décor, light, etc.)? Get as detailed as you can about what contributes to your energy so that you can design your classroom in ways that grows your energy. What do you notice about your energy in other areas of the school? How can you grow your energy in other ways and in other areas? What are ways that you can become more of an Energizer, or help others to become more so? What do you need to do or stop doing to improve or stop draining your energy?

≋

As with all the **Shifting Ground** moments in this book, you should feel free to alter or shift these activities to best represent who you are and how you enjoy thinking about creating a **Living Map**. For example, maybe you want to draw out an actual map with various islands. Each island might represent the continuum of languishing to flourishing, with a Burnout Island, an Island of Just Surviving, and a Flourishing Island, with other islands in between as you think through how you can express the different ways you engage in your work. At each island, you might have images of what it feels like to live there, and maybe you have activities, intentions, or expressions as routes toward each of the islands. This activity can be as involved and detailed as you like. The creative activity of making the **Living Map** can be done on your own, but it can also be done as a group of teachers—we did it with an entire district of school principals! The atmosphere in the room as these professionals enjoyed an afternoon of creativity, collaging their maps, and then recording each other on their phones to capture their intentions to follow their maps, was a joyful, lively, encouraging, and fun experience. Connecting with these teachers throughout the year, they let us know that they continued to use to the map to remind themselves of where they hoped to be heading throughout the year, and to also remember how they can shift their route and head away from burnout and toward flourishing (however they represented it). Because this had been a group activity, they also have colleague-friends who they could talk to about where they were on their maps, and could support each other to be moving towards their desired destination.

Notice how you feel as you pay attention to the thoughts and feelings that arise when engaged in your creative activity. Remember, there is no right way to be creative. As you listen to your Self, you are taking initiative to represent your learning as a step in your **Living Map**. Your map will be a unique representation of your journey through the inquiry in this book. We hope you'll share your map with others—both as you construct it and after you have finished. As you work your way through the inquiry in this book, you'll have opportunities to build up your map of flourishing and create the story of your journey. As you'll see, we offer suggestions for times to add to your map. We have tried to stay purposefully vague about how to create your map. You might find that you draw, paint or collage your journey of learning to flourish; perhaps you may choose a combination of all three.[1] Maybe you feel that you want to write a short story about your journey, creating characters to experience the journey as you learn. Whatever the modality for your expression, we know that the creative process will open new spaces for you to play and feel a sense of freedom to experiment in your learning. We encourage you to return to your representation of your **Living Map of Flourishing** at consistent points within this process.

1 On more that one occasion we've asked teachers (1-to-1 or in groups) to go on a photo-taking journey and take pictures of what they'd like to see more of (photo-voice or photo-diary method). They then assemble the pictures in a collage for sharing or personal reflection (or journaling).

A Flourishing Schools Perspective

We see flourishing as both an individual and a collective responsibility. Through this book we offer the argument that schools can be sites of human flourishing, and that focusing on personal thriving, as part of what it means to belong to a professional community, is an essential aspect of what it means to be a teacher. There have been significant shifts in the way we organize schools, away from the industrial, bureaucratic, and hierarchic model of school organization towards what has become understood as the learning community model, with increased attention paid to collaboration and collective leadership for school improvement. Using what we have learned from research in the positive sciences, research that we will share with you, we offer a different and complementary model of school organization and improvement in which we position ourselves with all others who see that we are at a critical point for re-imagining our society towards sustainability, social justice and freedoms, and personal wellbeing.

We hope to spark the imagination of practitioners and researchers towards the potential for deeper transformation of our school communities from places focusing on deficits to places of wellbeing, academic attainment, and nurturing of human capacities, capabilities, and potentials. As indicated, we do want to recognize the importance of academic achievement, and fully support the work of engaging students to attain their best in the educational outcomes that shape the curriculum and cultures in schools. We also think that the fixation with measurable outputs as evidence of effective schooling can all too often sideline and marginalize the importance of developing human capabilities for both students and teachers—a development that has implications and impacts for creating just, caring, and democratic societies (Apple & Beane, 2007; Giroux, 2015; Starratt, 2003)

If our students are to develop and grow to the fullest of their own potential, to explore and fill out their authentic selves as part of growing their communities, then we need to attend to the full experience of what it means to be human through schooling. We need to offer opportunities for them to build and grow their mental, emotional, physical, spiritual, relational, and ethical selves. This is a tall order to fill, and yet it is what teachers have always been called to do. What we are noticing as we attend to teacher wellbeing in schools, is that we have lost sight over the decades of the importance of supporting and encouraging teachers to fill out their highest potentials through their role as educator, and that to do this requires attention to their own mental, emotional, physical, spiritual, relational, and ethical growth in their professional role.

We aim to re-orient the focus of school improvement toward this call for fulfillment in and through teaching, a call that has been offered by many before us (Hansen, 2005; Higgins, 2011; Greene, 1978). Re-focusing our stories of schools towards a metaphor of human flourishing provides a shift in how we imagine the organization of schools as learning communities. The shift is toward noticing and attending to the positive human capabilities of the organization, such as love, courage, kindness, wisdom, and compassion.

We hold the view that schools can and ought to become increasingly positive human systems, and that vibrant learning communities can become the "vehicles for bringing more humanity, courage, wisdom, love and value into the world" (Cooperrider, nd). We affirm teachers and other school leaders who have long been recognized for their contributions to a more just, caring, democratic, and civil society (Giroux, 2015; Palmer, 2009; Starratt, 2004). There is a growing movement in popular culture towards enhancing compassion and care in our society, and a resurgence of attention to wellbeing and positive phenomena within schools. Fostering increasingly compassionate and life-giving learning communities is more probable when we focus on flourishing.

We will take up these ideas more fully in a later chapter. In the next chapter, we want to spend some time thinking with you about what it means to shift how we think about inquiry from something we "do," to thinking about inquiry as "a way of being as a learner." We have organized this book as a learning map, with both theory and practice offered to enrich your own thinking about what it means to flourish as an educator, and to show you the relevance for your own professional growth.

Paying attention to our stories as a way of noticing what works well is one way of shifting toward a flourishing mindset. In the next chapter we describe what it means to notice flourishing through engaging in the work of teaching as a living inquiry, a way of thinking about professional learning. We provide an overview of what it might mean to carry out an appreciative inquiry as a perspective for how to engage in a living inquiry of flourishing as an educator within a professional community.

Chapter Four

Noticing Through Attending to Story

In this chapter we offer you another **Heart Print** and invite you to engage in the **Shifting Ground** moments. These are opportunities for you to record your learning, as well as your ongoing questions and emerging intentions about what it means to you to flourish. This document is a living one, meaning that it will shift and change as you move along in your inquiry. There is no right way to design your **Living Map of Flourishing** and there is no right way to capture your learning. We think your map is initiated with the intention to improve fulfillment and fruitful practice, to grow your wellbeing. Again, this living document is a place for recording your learning, where you are generating knowledge and attuning to the new understandings you form as you connect with us, and hopefully your colleagues, to co-create your realities in ways that puts wellbeing at the heart of your work. We see this as a starting place for building a flourishing inquiry community as you engage with our theories and practices, learn to notice your own flourishing theories, and develop your own flourishing practices. As you move along in your journey we encourage you to test your map for authenticity and alignment with your beliefs, values, and deep intentions. Your map is YOUR explanation of your learning, of what influences you, and of what you hope to influence.

As you engage on this wellbeing journey, and as you document your learning on your **Living Map**, you will start to notice connections and patterns that become your anchoring guideposts for knowing you are attending to your thriving. There are fields of research and writing that you can use to inform and shape your guideposts, but the work of creating your map is not the process of adopting theories, swapping out fancier versions, borrowing models, or fully applying findings of experts that announce or identify flourishing. Rather, the kind of noticing we mean is connected to the work of contemplation, is deeply personal, and has a price tag (mainly set-aside time and self-patience). The work of creating your **Living Map of Flourishing** emerges from the practice and habit of noticing that which makes you feel most deeply 'you' in your work; what makes you feel alive, engaged, whole, connected, happy, and all the other positive qualities you may find as you dig in to your unique experience of flourishing.

What is Flourishing?

Earlier we asked the question, what is flourishing? There is no one right, perfectly clear description of what it means to flourish as an educator—this is an evolving personal and professional pursuit, with progress gained through our paying close attention to what makes us feel alive, connected, engaged, and well. Flourishing is defined from a psychological perspective as living "within an optimal range of human functioning, one that connotes goodness, generativity, growth, and resilience" (Fredrickson & Losada, 2005, p. 678). From a philosophical perspective, flourishing suggests virtuous living and the desired end toward which we strive as we aim to live a good life (Nussbaum, 1994; Rasmussen, 1999). In our research, teachers described many different ways of feeling that they are flourishing. Some teachers described the importance of laughing and finding fun moments with students and colleagues. Others described the importance of feeling that they belong to a team who share a deep commitment toward common goals for improving their students' experiences. Some mentioned that they feel a sense of flourishing when they remember to slow down and really be present with their students and colleagues, and be in the moment in their teaching. Others described how feeling like they're part of a family at work, when they make time to connect with each other and when they feel like they "know each other and have each others' backs" is central to what it means to them to flourish. We heard about the importance of finding balance in work and life, of making time for exercise, family, and friendships. There are as many ways of flourishing as there are individuals and groups within a school.

Noticing who you are and what makes you thrive within the various relationships and groups that make up the connected webs of relationships of your living system is the work of your flourishing inquiry.

Becoming curious about who you are, who you intend to become, and uncovering the true work and identity you associate with being a teacher are important aspects of this learning journey. Questions are an essential aspect of inquiry, and part of your work is learning to ask the questions that can guide you toward exploring the knowledge and practices that might lead you to the getting answers. We remember going to a small conference in Sweden and hearing the Director General for Education say: "We teach our students to know, to do, to be, and to dare." According to the program we were expecting him to speak for 45 minutes, but, instead, after this opening statement he then sat down and invited the moderator to see if there were any questions. Of course the definitional, "why" and "how" questions are all-important, but, in this instance, there was certainly no doubts about the succinctly anchored, articulated or chartered ends towards which that system was moving. Your flourishing inquiry is about delving deep into learning about what is most important to you and noticing what happens when you design ways to live out these important values, beliefs, and dreams more often in your work. Inquiry is more than asking and answering the right questions, it is a vital process of curiosity, investigation, exploration, openness and questing, researching and pursuing, enhanced by our involvement with others in the community (Kuklthau, Maniotes & Caspari, 2007).

Inquiry as Stance: Building our Living Theories for Flourishing

Let's expand on the idea that inquiry is more than asking and answering questions. We suggest that it can be understood as a way of engaging in and with the world, and of acknowledging the important role of those within the system to notice—and respond to—changing conditions in ways that grow and build knowledge and practice for continuously improving ourselves, our relationships, our work and our lives. This assumption of inquiry as a way of being, a stance we take in our work and life, is a way of recognizing and affirming knowledge generated by practitioners as integral and essential to building and growing the people and the profession. Inquiry as stance positions practitioners as knowers, and recognizes (honours and respects) the intellectual and wisdom capacity of practitioners:

> We regard inquiry as stance as a grounded theory of action that positions the role of practitioners and practitioner knowledge as central to the goal of transforming teaching, learning, leading, and schooling. We see inquiry as stance as a positive thesis that goes beyond mere critique of the current education regime and contributes to efforts to re-envision the work of practitioners in global societies. (Cochran-Smith & Lytle, 2009, p. 119)

Stance is about positioning, about creating a platform from which to live and be heard in the world. It is about positioning yourself as an inquiry educator, not by a sequence of steps or an experience connected to a certain time, but, rather, as a way of being.

This positioning is important as we think about engaging in an inquiry to learn about our own flourishing. As we engage with our colleagues to collaboratively theorize, internalize, and interiorize what it means to flourish, we build knowledge and practice that contribute to growing our own—and others'—practice, and the act of inquiring together provides opportunity for us to make sense of our work in ways that matter to us. This active meaning-making approach to our work and life, inquiry as stance, is strengthened when we engage with others in the process of re-imagining teaching and living as a more whole, appreciative, and positive experience of schooling for self and others.

Through this inquiry and meaning-making process we create an openness for noticing our tacit personal theories, narratives (scripts), and actions that we call our living theory, an evolving awareness and understanding gained through your ongoing inquiry into your beliefs, thoughts, actions, and practices. Living theories "express life affirming energy of individuals, cultures and the cosmos with values and understanding that is claimed to carry hope for the future of humanity" (Whitehead, 2008, p. 103). Whitehead (2008) suggested that living theory emerges from an inquiry into the influences that shape who we are as an educator as a way of moving toward ongoing improvement. We see claiming your living theory as a way of claiming your agency for growing self as part of a commitment toward improving, for all, the worlds within which you work and live. This is a lofty claim, but it resonates strongly with our beliefs about seeing the work of teaching as an investment in bettering humanity.

Developing living theory is a form of educator research, a professional practice that recognizes that "knowledge has many sources, and they are best honoured when they are used as part of a lively dialectic" (Allender & Allender, 2008). We offer our living theory of flourishing to you, through this book, as part of a lively conversation about wellbeing, intending that you will engage with it in unique ways that are best suited to you. However, we want to underline the importance of your personal and professional agency in testing and examining your own evolving living theory. Attending to how you language your experiences of reality is an important step toward developing an agency for wellbeing. Uncovering your living theory, and noticing your role in shaping your experiences, and those of your community, is a central component to living and growing wellbeing or happiness (as it is sometimes called). This process requires personal courage. Courage is necessary for looking into our beliefs and our taken-for-granted assumptions about how and why things work (or don't work). Of course, it makes sense to do this in an honest and fresh way. This isn't a new thing for most of us, but playing the comparison game or failing to challenge the comfortable-but-compromising false narratives in our personal and professional lives can be difficult. Providing a setting or climate for teachers to take on this personal development work of uncovering and attending to their story telling about their work is a powerful tool for creating communities where deep learning, growth, and even transformation can happen for both the teachers and their students.

Storytelling as a Tool for Reflection and Generation

Storytelling and the narrative truth threads that emerge from stories are grounded in the intimate aspect of our lives and represent some of the most profound ways that we humans have to describe, share, shape, and come to understand our experiences in the world (Baldwin, 2005; Clandinin & Connelly, 1996; Richardson, 2000). Humans share the tendency to make meaning from our experiences as we tell our stories about what we experience to ourselves and to each other. The idea that we shape our cultures by relaying and repeating stories about who we are, what we do, and how we behave is an important thread in our own research storyline. We see this thread emerging through most of our work with teachers, and certainly in the ways we engage with each other to share the stories we are catching. As you read more of our work, you won't be surprised to see that we describe and explain the power of storytelling in our work for us, and for teachers in general.

We believe that storytelling provides opportunity for self-understanding and shared understandings about the worlds we live in. The mere telling of a story creates our experience of reality, and so stories can be powerful tools for shaping human activity and organizations. In many ways, the best and the worst of the stories we tell about ourselves make us who we are. For example, in schools there are narratives present that define norms and standards of behaviour and that determine future courses of action (Weick, 1995). These stories shape our schools as communities, say a great deal about the work that we do within these organizations, and provide the markers for what and who is important to us. Most certainly there is a level of agency that we assume about how we experience reality and how we frame these experiences. From a positive psychology perspective, we might say that there is a "reflexive reality" (Seligman, 2011) that exists for each of us. Within this reality, we are able to shape our lives, for good or for bad, for right and for wrong, for virtue and for viciousness, all based on how we perceive, react to, and talk about our experiences. At a personal level, and at the level of the collective, the way we reflect on and talk about our experiences shapes the way we work, relate, and live (Cherkowksi & Walker, 2014).

We think that shifting how we think, imagine, feel and talk about communities in schools may shift how we perceive and experience the learning and growth that goes on in our lives, and those of others. Stories make up our descriptions and explanations of our practices, and our understanding of these are what we refer to as our living theory. Telling stories, and getting them listened to by others, is part of developing our flourishing maps. Our research stories are not usually our own stories, but they are a "story of stories" (McNiff, 2007, p. 5). In part, they are our own educator theory and they are also our reflection on our experiences—they are the result of our different ways of seeing, and the decisions we've made about what to focus our attention on and what to omit. On one occasion, Keith [and his wife Viv] put together a "here is your life" photo album for one of their four adult kids as a leaving home-base gift. Part way through the scanning and assembly project, it occurred to them that they had only taken pictures on the occasions of the best of times (clearly not fully representative of all the times), and that the project was thoroughly marked as a parental perspective on the son's life, rather than what might have been the young person's way of seeing the world. As a result the gift was accompanied with an acknowledgement of the futility of creating narratives for others with the claim of universal perspective on reality (even if well-intended).

Through our own lives, and in our work and research, we have seen how it is so important to see that our images can be distorted and slanted by the way others have framed our lives and our living. In this next **Heart Print** moment, we provide a story that we have shared often for its powerful message about the importance of paying attention to that which we wish to grow. We encourage you to read, take time to reflect, and then jot down impressions, ideas, and questions that emerge for you as you think of your agency in telling and interpreting stories. When you're ready, record on your map the influences of this **Heart Print** on your living theory. We encourage you to find ways to notice through the course of a day, a week, a month, and so on, how you listen to the many stories you tell and are told, and the ways that you respond to these many stories that script our lives. Keep recording your learning from your inquiry on your **Living Map**.

Heart Print

We like using this story, one we have seen in many places and with different characters (in this case it is a grandfather talking to his grandson), to illustrate our theories about the power of language and stories to shape our attitudes and behaviors: 'A fight is going on inside me,' he said to the boy. 'It is a terrible fight and it is between two wolves. One is evil - he is anger, envy, sorrow, regret, greed, arrogance, self-pity, guilt, resentment, inferiority, lies, false pride, superiority, and ego.' He continued, 'The other is good - he is joy, peace, love, hope, serenity, humility, kindness, benevolence, empathy, generosity, truth, compassion, and faith. The same fight is going on inside you - and inside every other person, too.' The grandson thought about it for a minute and then asked his grandfather, 'Which wolf will win?' The old man simply replied, 'The one you feed.'

Like the wise grandfather, we know that attending to strengths, virtues and positive outlooks, as opposed to a deficit-thinking, can increase resilience, vitality and happiness, and can lead to decreased stress, anxiety and depression (Lyubomirsky, King, & Diener, 2005). The question that is central to your flourishing inquiry makes your personal and professional wellbeing the foundation from which to then figure out, with others, how your wellbeing, and that of others, might likewise be supported to thrive. We all know that life is hard; it is unfair, it can be ugly and it is unevenly experienced. It was Max DePree (1989) who said the first task of a leader is to define reality, and the last task is to say thank you. We know that no amount of rose-coloured glasses, doses of idealism, nor abundance of wishful thinking can radically alter the harsh realities that regularly visit upon our lives, and the lives of those we love. We can, and do, feel marginalized, disenfranchised, despairing, lonely, and many other ways we co-experience the vulnerabilities of feeling less than fully human. Perhaps the image of a problem-less human is a fantasy. Perhaps, as Jean Vanier (2003; 2008) reminded us, becoming human is about facing, engaging, and embracing the challenges, and loving those who suffer disadvantage and unfairness.

There are light and dark sides of a real life. We do not know what the level of depth of your suffering is, because each of us experience suffering in different ways. We do not want to trivialize the pain and the inner anguish of those who suffer, and we know that even those who give the appearance of peacefulness and wellbeing may, in fact, be experiencing pain in their lives; pain that remains hidden because our organizations often demand that we keep our suffering to ourselves. However, we do see that we can take small steps to shift toward a more compassionate stance for ourselves, and for others with whom we work and live. What we can do is to notice how we talk to ourselves, and to others, about our experiences. We can encourage one another to be curious about how our responses to our perceived realities influence how we think and feel, and what we do in our work and in our life. We were moved by a story from one of our study participants about how he had made a decision to be more open and accepting in his work and life, so that he could be more responsive with his students and colleagues. He made a choice to respond to his environment in a new way and shared that his teaching experiences shifted the moment he recognised that "teaching is like improv acting. I learn to say 'yes' to what is in front of me." This small story highlights for us what it means to accept your agency in shaping your social realities—his agency is reflected through his playful spirit of engaging with the students, his colleagues, and the content in a more accepting way; learning to say 'yes' with an open heart.

Of course, the human spirit is complex, and we suggest that fundamental questions of personhood, identity, and attention to what gives life (and what depletes it) are crucial to our work as teachers. As you will find through charting your **Living Map**, noticing and examining your own stories and your own ways of responding, and unpacking the taken-for-granted assumptions that create the structure of your reality, can be powerful tools for constructing (with others) the futures you desire in your work. These activities of reflection can result in an experience of reality that more closely aligns with a potential for generative and positive growth that we seek to create and sustain in ourselves and others in our school community.

Appreciative Inquiry: A Brief Overview

Part of developing your **Living Map of Flourishing** is learning to appreciate what you do, who you are, and who you intend to be. This is another common thread in our research story about flourishing in schools; you will find this next thread woven through most, if not all, of our writing and presenting on our research on flourishing. We use ideas from appreciative inquiry (AI) as an explanatory tool for the power of positive change, and as a practical tool as a method for engaging with self and other toward the positive change that we most desire in our work and life. We see the many benefits and possibilities for AI to encourage the development of positive, appreciative, generative conditions in schools where teachers, students, staff, and all other community members may flourish.

AI was originally developed for use as an organizational development tool for instigating and carrying out change (Cooperrider & Srivasta, 1987). Over the years, this process intelligence has been adapted and adopted for use, across sectors, with small teams and with individuals. The AI practices may shift for each initiative and context, so we won't go into great detail about the practicalities of an appreciative inquiry. However, there are several underpinning principles that we believe are important to understand as we think together about what it means to inquire from an appreciative stance.

First, the process was developed from a **social constructionist** perspective that assumes that we, ourselves, originate and construct our realities. We do so as we interpret the many different stories we hear ourselves telling about our evolving selves and our perspectives about the world around us (Gergen, 2015). For AI, this means an understanding that reality is co-created, in the moment, by all who participate in the process—and that there can be multiple realities for participant observers. This also means that recognition is given to the language we use to create reality. So it is important to be intentional, inclusive, and to value differences, throughout the AI process. A second principle is that of **simultaneity**. This principle reflects the belief that the act of inquiry and the act of change are not separate moments, but in fact happen at the same time. This means that the act of asking questions actually influences the hearer, or the group. In light of this, the AI process ensures that positive and generative questions guide the inquiry. Based on this principle, it is also important to recognize that what we focus on tends to become our reality, and so, again, asking positive questions to elicit generative conversations about positive possibilities is an important principle for an AI process. You'll have guessed by now that we are taking you through some of these principles to prepare you for some implementation!

The **poietic principle**[2] recognizes that how we story, or author, our reality reflects what is most important to us. AI change processes are carefully guided to support participants through a positive authoring of their organizational change and transformation processes. Similarly, the **anticipatory principle** is related in that it supports the belief that how we think about our future shapes the way we move toward that future. From this, an important assumption supporting AI is that carrying forward parts of the past can help groups move forward more comfortably into the future. As a consequence, the parts carried forward should be from the best aspects of the organizational or personal past. Finally, AI is grounded in the belief that we can be more deeply engaged in an inquiry through **positive questions** that enable us to focus our energy

2 Yes, we've spelled "poietic" or "poiesis" correctly. We derive our word from this Greek word, which means "to create" or "that which leads to a thing becoming" ("leading into being").

on those parts of the organization that nourish us, that gives us energy, that make us feel most alive. These principles and accompanying assumptions reflect the shifting understanding about organizations and people as living systems, as opposed to machine-like bureaucracies or functionaries with strict hierarchies, stringent rules, predictable fates and reward systems (Reed, 2007; Whitney & Trosten Bloom, 2010).

We see the possibilities for engaging in schools from positions and platforms of gratefulness, openness and freshness, and we see this as quite easily mediated through learning about how an appreciative process can awaken teachers to what is best in themselves and in the systems that they co-create through their relationships at work.

Heart Print

As you read this quote from the original creators of appreciative inquiry, imagine how your work might shift if you embraced an appreciative approach to inquiry in your work:

Reading the world gratefully...embracing the sacredness or miracle of life on this planet for its intimations of something more and for what's next or possible is a fundamental part of the call for an AI of valuing those things of value worth valuing. It's also a key to spirit of inquiry that is moving from the edges of the known to the unknown (mystery) in ways that broadens and opens minds, ignites real curiosity and expansive questions, and inspires fresh images of possibility. (Cooperrider & Srivasta, 2013, pp. 5-6)

As you think about this quote, what do you imagine as possibilities for you as an educator, and for your professional learning community as part of a school? What might it feel like to teach from a place of passion, a place of strength, from a place of knowing that when you engage in your strengths you feel most deeply yourself and want to share this best self with others? What are you moved to record on your **Living Map?**

What are your strengths and how can you live those out in your work? We encourage you to spend some time thinking about what it means to inquire from an appreciative stance into your work and life. Take some time to list your passions, your dreams and your strengths. Maybe you feel moved to share these with your friends and colleagues; perhaps talk about how they see you already living these out in your work and life and how you can be supported to keep doing so. What happens in your work when you embrace the mystery of your work and life? There are so many questions that can guide you. We encourage you to take time to listen for the questions that are most meaningful for you, that guide you on your flourishing inquiry, knowing that these questions will shift and change as you move along your learning journey.

Research in psychology shows that owning our strengths (and, of course, this requires knowing what they are), and finding new ways to use these strengths often in our work and life, is one way of increasing and sustaining happiness (Seligman, 2011). An educator who increasingly finds ways to work in their sweet spots is highly likely to be a happy and healthy educator. In the next **Shifting Ground** moment we offer you an experience of an AI process using questions from our research with teachers.

Shifting Ground

Who Am I when I Am at my Best?
Think to a time (in teaching or in other aspects of your life) when you felt you were living out the 'real you' with a feeling of excitement and energy. A time when you felt you wanted to find new ways to keep doing these things that made you feel alive, engaged, and inspired. From that appreciative and strengths-based perspective, answer the following questions in as much detail as you can:

- What were you doing?
- Why were you doing these things?

- Who were you with, or who helped you to engage in these ways?
- What did you feel as you engaged in these activities and ways of being?

Bring your full awareness and all your senses to these questions (take them one by one and give each time to settle and benefit from your full attention).

- In these times what did you see, feel, hear, and even taste?
- What do you notice about you and others are talking, sharing, expressing feelings and ideas?

As you recall your narrative, think back to a time as an educator when you felt these experiences. Describe and detail what was going on (inside and out).

Now, imagine you had a magic wand and could create anything you wanted or needed to develop an environment that would foster and support this greatest version of you as a teacher.

- What would you create?
- What would it look like for you to live out that expression of who you are when you are at your best?
- What is one small thing you could do right now to live out that expression of who you are in your teaching?
- Who is one person with whom you would like to share this appreciative inquiry? What is one small step that expresses your commitment to getting more of what fits you best?

≋

As you think about this appreciative inquiry experience, what stories of past experiences or dreams of your future are you inspired to share? Jot them down in as much detail as you can. As you reflect back on your notes, take some time to add to your **Living Map** what you have learned about who you are when you are at your best, some of the conditions that help to foster and support that version of yourself, and the small steps that you will take right away to move closer to that version of yourself in your current work. Be sure to jot down who else you will share this with so that you might continue to build a community of colleagues to support and help each other grow toward flourishing.

Your inquiry into flourishing will evolve through the development of your **Living Map**; specifically as you reflect on what you are noticing as you pay attention to the questions you are asking about building your wellbeing. By the way, your map of just scraping by, suffering, living in a state of perpetual exhaustion, self-depreciating, and struggling will also develop if that is what you give attention to (or perhaps even as a default process). Your **Living Map of Flourishing** is your documentation of educator knowledge. Each of our maps will be unique, and they will also be relationally grounded. We know that teaching is not a solo endeavour. We teach within living systems built as webs of interconnected and interdependent relationships. Learning happens within and from these relationships, so our theories of practice and living are constructed as part of what it means to belong to communities with others. As with all sections in this book, this chapter can be explored personally, or as a group. Perhaps you have a group of people (for example, drawn from parents, teachers, community members, and administrators) who are already interested in engaging in these conversations with you. We hope that as you work through these materials, you will start to bring together a community of inquiry that both affirms and challenges your journey; one that supports care, love, and compassion, and the courage needed to look deeply into who you are, to who you intend to become (as individuals and as a group), and to inquire into your true work as teachers. Collectively reflecting on your own learning can lead to new learning, which, in turn, will inform future action. We hope that belonging to, and contributing to, a flourishing learning community (either through this book or in conjunction with one you have created in your local community) will provide you and your colleagues with a sense of collective responsibility to, and engagement with, each other as you share your stories of experiences.

As we described, your work in this inquiry is to become an expert in building your own knowledge about being the teacher you are meant to be. It is partly about your influence within that educator work, as well as your part in the processes of engaging with others in a professional learning community. Your living theory of educator practice is an emerging one. This is an evolving theory about what best reflects your beliefs, experiences, and understandings. It is about the core values that you hold about what it means to teach, to learn, to connect with others in pursuit of improving your practice. It is about your determined pursuit of the higher purpose of contributing to the deepening and enriching of our common humanity. Teaching is lofty work, and we mean that in the most reverential way possible. It is not a stretch to call being a teacher sacred work. As you explore your **Living Map** of your learning about what it means to flourish, we hope you come to appreciate and honour the core purposes that originally drew you to teaching, and to those purposes that currently keep you energized to be an educator. Learning to notice what makes you feel alive and whole in your work and life is an important habit for growing more wellbeing, and is a lovely practice to model for others as a way to encourage them to notice their flourishing.

Appreciative inquiry is a strengths-based model of thinking and reflecting on action for change. AI capitalizes on accessing a positive core of beliefs to serve as motivating images for creating a desired or preferred future. Using appreciative inquiry through the use of positive questions can become a powerful practice of personal, professional, and community transformation. As always, this practice is even more powerful when done in community. We invite you to continue to experiment with this powerful tool for transformation. We know that you will adapt and adopt AI as needed, based on your growing awareness of your living theory of flourishing. As you uncover your positive core, beliefs, and actions you'll see what is authentically aligned with who you are intend to be. You'll find yourself setting up opportunities for using your strengths throughout the day, and naturally (by new nature) carrying out appreciative inquiries with your colleagues to continue to journey toward flourishing. Engaging in a flourishing inquiry means noticing what makes you thrive so that you may grow more of that in your work and life. As we will describe in the next chapter, growing wellbeing can happen as you nurture conditions for flourishing through building knowledge that supports your ongoing learning and growth, and through building practices, routines, structures, and processes that foster wellbeing as the core aspect of your work as a teacher.

Chapter Five

Nurturing through Growing Knowledge and Developing Competencies

Intentionally focusing your inquiry to notice what works well helps you come alive, and contributes to your feeling whole, connected, and engaged in your work. A focus on what is working for you is an important practice for putting wellbeing at the centre of your work as a teacher. This habit of noticing flourishing can be powerful and transformative; however, this habit requires that you nurture flourishing through building knowledge and practice that sustains you in your noble pursuit of teaching. Part of developing your **Living Map of Flourishing** entails developing an awareness of theory and practice of wellbeing as a foundation. We think the adage that good theory produces good practice for good theory holds true.

Our current theorizing about flourishing emerged from research in positive psychology, positive organizational scholarship and school improvement. As we linked together our thinking about the alignment and potentials of these findings for the work of teachers, we then connected our ongoing research of flourishing with our knowledge about learning community theory. The conceptual model that we offer here has resonated with teachers in the field. They have seen this visual representation as a useful heuristic for reflecting on individual and collective wellbeing, and as a practical tool for noticing, nurturing, and sustaining the conditions that contribute to what it means to be whole, engaged, and alive in our work. In this chapter we unpack the model for you, referring to our previous writing to bring to life each domain and to the virtues that make up this model.

A Conceptual Model for Flourishing in Schools

Drawn by the influence of positive psychology and positive organizational studies, we developed a conceptual model for flourishing in schools (see Figure 5.1) that is underscored by a holistic view of the development of human capacity (Nussbaum, 2011; Scheffler, 1985; Sen, 2009) from a learning community perspective. This model has high resonance for teachers, especially as their role is conceived as creating space for their own and others' flourishing. We identify three intersecting domains of attention: (1) Subjective Wellbeing; (2) Leaderful Mindsets; and (3) Adaptive Community. Together they provide the foundation for exploring the phenomenon of flourishing. While the main emphasis of this Teacher Wellbeing book is obviously on the subjective wellbeing of teachers, we think the wellbeing of everyone in the school setting is crucial to the school being a flourishing community. Our research also gives attention to leaderful mindsets and adaptive communities. We will describe these elements and show how these help us design, create, and develop generative workplaces. In our view, the hosting virtues and dynamics of compassion, trust, and hope combine and interact to evoke the nexus between flourishing schools and flourishing persons.

Figure 5.1. Conceptual Model for Flourishing in Schools

This model reflects our belief in the saying that "the school consists of the people who walk into the building everyday." Sometimes we forget that schools are people, not just brick and mortar buildings. Later in this chapter we elaborate on the various aspects of this conceptualization, but first we need to provide a brief overview of the research fields of positive psychology and positive organizational scholarship that influenced our development of this model. Given the importance we have placed on building your living theory as a way of growing your own sense of flourishing, we provide **Heart Print** and **Shifting Ground** moments throughout the chapter for you to reflect on your experiences of flourishing in relation to the theories that underpin the model.

Positive Psychology

Martin Seligman is often seen as the seminal animator and progenitor of the movement towards positive psychology. Seligman's early work on authentic happiness and optimism (2002, 1998) made a significant impact on the study of how humans can maximize their happiness and lead more fulfilling lives. More recently, his work shifted to encompass a fuller understanding of what it means to live a good life, moving beyond the notion of seeking happiness toward a construct he calls wellbeing (Seligman, 2011). In simple terms, wellbeing is about a search for human flourishing where we attend to our strengths in five areas: positive emotion, engagement, relationships, meaning, and achievement. These five elements of wellbeing are intimately linked to teachers' work in schools and lie at the heart of what it means to be a student and learner.

As we have tended to describe, positive psychological practices encourage the development of positive outlooks, habits, and mental models and focus on describing and building positive qualities in persons rather than trying to repair the negative and destructive ones (Achor, 2011; Ben-Shahar, 2008; Seligman, 2002). Positive psychology is the study of the conditions, strengths, and virtues—the study of what goes right in life—that enable persons and communities to thrive (Bakker & Schaufeli, 2008; Keyes, Fredrickson, & Park, 2012). In general, traditional views have focused on "deficit models;" whereas positive psychology uses a "strengths-based" lens (Seligman & Csikszentmihalyi, 2000).

This paradigm shift in psychological perspective aims to foster a full life of positive growth, rather than trying to simply reduce or relieve misery. Seligman explained that traditional psychological counselling tended to leave his clients empty—reduced of misery but not necessary fulfilled or capable of finding fulfillment. While positivity will not overcome everything, positive psychology provides research-informed encouragement for us to learn how to exert influence where we are able to do so, through our perceptions and expectations, in order to shift our experiences of our social reality. We see many possibilities for transferring and translating findings from positive psychology to the work of teachers. Positive psychology is committed to uncovering the varied ways that humans tap into a greater sense of wellbeing in their lives through attending to personal strengths and positive growth towards a sense of flourishing (Seligman, 2011). In our other writing we have shared how experiences that increase peoples' feelings of positive emotion will improve their wellbeing by buttressing their physical, social, mental, and psychological resources (Diener, 2000; Fredrickson, 2008; Fredrickson & Losada, 2005). People who flourish experience the opposite of languishing, yearning for more, or feelings of being stuck in a rut (Keyes & Lopez, 2002). People who flourish are more resilient and come closer to self-fulfillment, contentment, and happiness (Haybron, 2008; Martin & Marsh, 2006; Rassmussen, 1999).

Positive Organizational Scholarship

During the time when positive psychology was growing its roots as a research area within the field of psychology, there was also an emerging stream of research in business and management fields that paid attention to similar concepts of positivity, and to the human capabilities within various organizations. These researchers explained that at a time when deficit thinking seemed to be infusing everything from politics, to business, to schools, strengths-based leadership and management were increasingly sought (Cameron & Caza, 2004; Cameron, Dutton, & Quinn, 2003). David Cooperrider, who developed appreciative inquiry, noted that positive organizational development is "centrally about the design of *positive institutions* that not only elevate and connect human strengths (internally) but serves to refract and magnify our highest human strengths into society" (Cooperrider & Godwin, 2011, p. 738).

Grounded in the recognition of a need for building and sustaining organizations from a strengths-based perspective, positive organizational scholarship responded to a desire in the practice and scholarship of organization and management to view human interactions within the organization in a virtuous way. Pace (2010) described this new scholarship as a different way of exploring why certain organizations perform so much better than others, and explained that "concepts about virtue, compassion, and positivity may seem simple but they turn out to be crucial elements for broader success" (p. 1). From our work with teachers, we have noticed the impact of attending to school organizations from a positive, appreciative perspective, and have seen and experienced how the intentional act of seeking out the virtuous qualities within an organization can lead to increasing organizational virtuousness (Cameron, 2003), individually and collectively. We see how practices developed from research in positive psychology and positive organizational research can encourage personal professional growth at work, and think that this positive shift in school organizations could become an innovative approach for improving professional learning and flourishing for teachers and other school leaders.

Unpacking the Flourishing in Schools Model

As indicated, we have been influenced by research and writing across a variety of fields and disciplines. As we were connecting with teachers in the field to learn more about what how they understood what it meant to flourish in schools, we were exploring research and writing in psychology, business, and sociology to develop a broader lens for how educational researchers and practitioners might shift the view of schools away from a deficit-model approach, or a "problem-to-be fixed" approach, and toward a more whole, positive, and human-development view. In this next section we provide an overview of the scholarship that informed the development of our model, and invite you to reflect on how this model resonates with the ways you have experienced, or hope to experience, your own work in schools. We start with the domain that reflects the main focus of this book, subjective wellbeing.

Subjective Wellbeing

Finding a way to capture all that is meant by wellbeing can be very challenging, and so we decided to highlight a few aspects of research in positive psychology that captures how teachers were describing what it meant to experience subjective wellbeing in their work: positive emotions, positive relationships, a sense of making a difference, and their experience of meaningful or purposeful work. We found that positive relationships were central to how teachers experience a sense of flourishing. They flourished when they had opportunities to provide and receive care, charity, compassion for and with others, as well as having some fun and connecting in ways that made them feel they belonged to a team, or even a family, of people who were all working towards something good and important together. For teachers, wellbeing was a highly relational process, and the experience of wellbeing in community was a way to share, accelerate, sustain, transform, and even multiply their own experiences of wellbeing.

Diener and Seligman (2004) described wellbeing as "people's positive evaluation of their lives, which includes positive emotion, engagement, satisfaction, and meaning" (p. 1). From findings in positive psychology, we understand that a focus on positive emotions in one aspect of life can contribute to increasing capacities and capabilities in other areas of our lives (Fredrickson, 2008). As was learned from the research in positive organizations, achieving a level of positivity in the workplace has generative, life-giving, and beneficial effects across many levels of the workplace. Given that the focus of this book is on teacher wellbeing, we offer a more detailed description of wellbeing than of the other aspects of the model. We outline below research-informed descriptions of several qualities or characteristics of wellbeing at work—job satisfaction, income and wellbeing, social contact, and wellbeing.

The Structure of Wellbeing

The domains of a teacher's life (e.g., satisfaction with classroom work, friends, and relationships) that are closest and most immediate to a teacher's personal life are those that most influence that teacher's subjective wellbeing. Satisfaction in a teacher's life may depend on the culture, beliefs, and way that the teacher's life is structured. One's subjective well-being is determined by a large number of factors. Diener (1984) wrote that, "Variables from the weather to beliefs to interactions between personality and environment will probably play a part, and it is unrealistic that any one will be prepotent" (p. 37). Researchers have shown that, despite the effects of personality on attitudes toward work, it appears that teachers'—and general worker—satisfaction depends on characteristics of the workplace. Researchers found "that job stressors produce strain in teachers beyond the strain explained by temperament" (Diener & Seligman, 2004, pp. 222, 225).

There are a host of factors that contribute to job satisfaction. With others, Diener and Seligman concluded that rewarding jobs tend to have the following characteristics:

- Opportunity for personal growth
- Opportunity for using skills
- Variety of tasks
- Physical security
- Supportive supervisor
- Respect and high status
- Interpersonal contact
- Good pay and fringe benefits
- Clear requirements and information on how to meet them.

Job satisfaction can affect home-life satisfaction and vice versa. Researchers have found that marital quality and job satisfaction are related in that, "positive experiences at work reduced conflictual marital interactions that day, and conflictual marital interactions reduced the positivity of work experience the next day" (p. 224). In addition, those who are employed in jobs where there is lack of control experience lack of energy on non-workdays.

In the area of **income,** there is evidence that shows a positive relationship between income and subjective wellbeing. Unsurprisingly, Easterlin (1974) discovered that, within any given country, wealthier persons were happier than poorer persons.

Some studies have found a positive correlation between **age** and general satisfaction (including work satisfaction). Younger respondents reported stronger levels of both positive and negative satisfaction effect, but older subjects reported greater levels of overall happiness. From his early research, Diener stated, "young persons appear to experience higher levels of joy, but older persons tend to judge their lives in more positive ways" (1984, p. 28). He also reported that, "family and marriage satisfaction was the strongest predictor of [subjective wellbeing] in many studies" (p. 30). However, it is interesting to note that when parenthood and subjective wellbeing are studied together, the results are negligible or show negative effects.

Social contact increases one's subjective wellbeing. Being an extravert correlates with positive affect. More than being an extravert, it is the social engagement piece that positively affects happiness. However, the question of causality may run both ways. Diener (1984) wrote, "It could be that when people are happier, they are more sociable. It could be... that there is a bidirectional influence between sociability and happiness" (p. 31). Satisfaction with one's love life is strongly related to subjective wellbeing. One study found "that love was the most important resource for happiness" (p. 32).

A substantial number of studies show a relationship between **self-rated health** and subjective wellbeing. Not only is feeling good an important contributor to happiness, but good health enables individuals to do the things they want. Poor sleep has been related to unhappiness, and the question of direction of causality applies here also considering that, as Diener asserted, "it seems probable that the influence could be bi-directional" (p. 36). In addition, exercise is related to higher mood and happiness.

Learning to experience wellbeing more often. Over the years there has been an increasing interest in research about how to improve the positive psychological states of people. Findings indicate that our happiness is malleable – that we can improve or reduce our own happiness through various practices, activities, and states of mind. For example, Sonya Lyubomirsky's (2007) research findings indicated that up to forty percent of our happiness can be significantly shifted based on engaging in practices that have been found to increase states of happiness. While engaging in these practices do not substantially alter our fundamental personality, there is a large chunk of our disposition that we can control and choose to shift one way or the other. For example, in Lyubomirsky's research, she found that individuals who perform random acts of kindness, who set and meet challenging goals, and who spend a lot of time engaged in planning for happy experiences (such as holidays), and then reflect on the memories of these experiences, rate higher on happiness tests.

Other practices that can increase happiness include taking time to regularly reflect on moments and people for which we are grateful. Seligman (2011) found that taking this a step further and writing a letter to someone to express your gratitude, and then visiting that person to express that gratitude, significantly increased a person's sense of happiness. Researchers on positive emotions have found that engaging in experiences where you feel a positive emotion can carry over into other aspects of your life, where you will reap the benefits of increasing capacities such learning and connecting with others. So, it would seem that paying attention to when we feel good and creating opportunities, when possible, for these to happen at work has proven beneficial. Listening is an important piece of emotional support as this behaviour elevates one's sense of wellbeing and provides validation of persons (Jones, 2011). Palmer (2007) reminded us that if we want to grow as teachers, we must risk talking to one another about our inner life and be brave enough to 'wear our hearts on our sleeve' at work.

While the findings from research in positive psychology show that happiness is a part of flourishing, wellbeing encompasses more than feeling positive emotions and experiences. Wellbeing is a more complex construct that includes the importance of positive relationships, a sense of meaning, purpose, and accomplishment as parts of what it means to flourish (Seligman & Diener, 2004; Seligman, 2011). Of course wellbeing may be framed at personal, interpersonal, community, and society levels; all are important and interact to constitute overall wellbeing. In this next section we will give attention to interpersonal and community wellbeing.

Adaptive Community: Relationships at Work

This is a second domain in the flourishing schools model. Humans are a social species; we are meant to live, to work, and to play together in social arrangements. Learning to be in relationships with others is a developed skill. Historically, teaching has been described as a lonely job, where teachers carry out their work in their classrooms, isolated from one another (Lortie, 1975). With the growing trend to develop schools as learning communities for attaining school improvement goals, creating opportunities for teachers to work together in professional relationships, in the form of collaboration, shared reflection, and shared decision-making, is an important aspect of school organizing. Coupled with this is the growing need to understand how to foster climates for improved professional learning (Hargreaves & Fullan, 2012).

We developed the construct of Adaptive Community (Cherkowski & Walker, 2014; Cherkowski et al., 2018) in ways that link to ideas of resiliency and self-aware, context-sensitive, emergent, living systems (Capra, 2004; Heifetz, Grashow & Linksy, 2009; Senge, 2006). We know that students (and teachers) do their best learning in supportive, compassionate, and caring environments (Schonert-Reichl & Hymel, 2007), and we have thought about how to develop new ways of thinking about community from a positive perspective in education (Cherkowski & Walker, 2014). From research on professional development, we know that it can be helpful to implement strategies that create challenging, but emotionally safe, climates for improving professional learning for teachers (Drago-Severson, 2009). We have noticed how positive organizational research may have transferability for supporting professional learning and development in school organizations. For example, individual and group resiliency has been found to increase as the capacity to constructively express emotions is nurtured in work relationships (Stephens, Heaphy, Carmeli & Dutton, 2013). This idea of resiliency is echoed in our concept of adaptive community; an environment where teachers and other school leaders are encouraged and supported in learning how to communicate openly and effectively with colleagues, to disagree respectfully, to encourage creativity and risk-taking for self and others, to develop healthy work teams and to disband teams that are no longer working well, to provide and receive compassion and care at work, to draw out passion, fun, and joy in themselves and in others at work. This story, provided to us by a participant in our research, represents a vibrant example of what it means to flourish as a member of an adaptive community (Cherkowski & Walker, 2014). This imagined story of flourishing resonated, for us, with the ideas of resilience, connectedness, hope, and joy at work:

> The scene: a crowded staffroom after a rigorous debate about a student-learning-related matter. The crowd is inclusive: administrators, teachers, support staff. What do you see? People mingling. One sign on the whiteboard reminds folks that next Tuesday is "Soup Day" and asks who will be bringing the food. Another sign reminds everyone of a future staff party (organized by the school custodian), which is going to be a cross-country ski event followed by a wine and cheese get-together at a teacher's cabin. What do you hear? Engaged, respectful conversation. Laughter—lots of it. What do you taste? Plates of homemade chocolate chip cookies brought by the PAC [parent advisory committee] with a note, "thanks for caring so much about our kids."

This description of a flourishing school resonates with the key ideas of positive emotions and relationships, which are at the core of our learning and growing. For us, adaptive communities collectively learn their way forward in ongoing improvement with a deliberate focus on nurturing positive relationships and wellbeing. This attention seems to grow the structures and flexibilities needed to respond to their dynamic learning environments with creativity, curiosity, and appreciation (Cherkowski, Hanson & Walker, 2018). Often the question becomes, who are the people who generate and sustain these types of learning communities? Who are the ones who navigate and make sense of the relationships, roles, and reliances within a school? We suggest that shared or distributed leadership and authentic teamship can make "the difference."

Leaderful Mindsets: Connecting Leading to Meaning

Leaderful Mindsets is the third domain of the flourishing in schools model. Learning how to make sense of our work and life in ways that highlight and promote how we are striving (with others) toward work that is meaningful, and that fulfills a purpose, can help us to feel that we belong and contribute to something greater than ourselves. This is an important element for the promotion of personal and collective well-being (Lyubomirsky, 2007; Seligman, 2011). Many teachers intuitively know that their contribution to their students has meaning. We would add that finding ways to see themselves and their colleagues as important pieces of a larger whole, all working together toward meaningful and purpose-driven ends, is a powerful opportunity for growing a sense of flourishing. From our participants we learned that teachers who thrive feel that they are an important part of a team working towards meaningful, shared purposes. These teachers deeply enjoy and appreciate opportunities for shared leadership and knowing that they are an important part of making the school a flourishing one for all their students, staff, and community members (Cherkowski & Walker, 2016). We suggest that leadership can be understood as a mindset; one where teachers often engage as leaders to contribute to improving the school for students and all others. Finding ways to see and make connections to how their work contributes to the larger, shared goals provides a greater sense of agency and ownership for engaging in further shared leadership. Developing the capacities and dispositions for this mindset of being a shared contributor to improving the schools seemed to provide more immediate feelings of contribution and wellbeing through the work of teaching and learning (Cherkowski & Walker, 2016). In our model, the Leaderful Mindset domain reflects the educational research findings that ensuring capacity for sustainable school improvement means that the capacity to lead must be fostered at many levels of the school (Elmore, 2000; Hargreaves & Fullan, 2012; Slater, 2008). We suggest that a school full of leaders is a good thing (thus "leaderful"). The research findings from positive psychology indicate that wellbeing increases with autonomy and a positive sense of achievement (Seligman, 2011), as each member (students, staff, and teachers) takes their turn leading, following and contributing with passion, promise, and purpose.

In his research on learning communities in schools, Keith observed that positive role modeling throughout a school can lead to a vibrancy and a school full of leaders (Sackney & Walker, 2007). Ensuring capacity for sustainable school improvement and elevated levels of wellbeing means that formal leaders must develop leaderful capacity at many levels of the school (Elmore, 2000; Slater, 2008). Elsewhere this has been referred to as shared, dispersed, plural, or distributed leadership.

An example of how we understand the Leaderful Mindset domain is depicted in Robin Sharma's (2010) business fable, *The Leader Who Had No Title*. A young bookstore clerk undertook a great learning journey with a magical mentor to come to understand that leadership is a role available to all. It is understood that through pursuing personal leadership in all aspects of our work, we can transform any job into a meaningful career that serves others and brings enormous personal satisfaction. And, of course, the profits will likely follow. We see how there is much to be learned from thinking about the power and potential of transforming classrooms and schools through developing capacities and habits of mind that reflect a personal leadership approach to creating meaningful work. Robert Quinn (1996) wrote about the potential for transformation in self, and then others, when work becomes an opportunity for personal and professional development. We suggest that classrooms and schools can serve as similar places of personal and professional transformation through developing positive climates that support meaningful personal growth toward increasing leaderful mindsets in schools. In the last chapter of this book, we address the importance of the formal building leaders in the school for supporting a focus on teacher wellbeing.

Nurturing Professional Virtues: Compassion, Trust, and Hope

As you can see in our model (Figure 5.1), we have indicated that there are three professional virtues that exist as elements all of the domains. These virtues are compassion, hope, and trust. From our own research with educational leaders, we know that these three virtues are essential catalysts for positive relationships and ethical decision-making in schools (Cherkowski, 2012; Cherkowski, Kutsyuruba & Walker, 2015). We know that teaching and learning are relational experiences, and that these experiences are best encouraged and supported in conditions where students and teachers feel safe, cared for, respected, and engaged. Given these understandings about the relational nature of both teaching and learning, our emerging flourishing theory includes knowledge and learning gained from research in positive organizational scholarship about the important influence and impact of focusing on the virtuous aspects of organizations (c.f., Cameron & Caza, 2004; Dutton, 2003; Quinn, 2015). The research insights gained from their research on building and maintaining healthy organizations has informed our thinking about the role of the professional virtues of compassion, hope, and trust in how we conceive of flourishing teachers in flourishing schools. We have also been influenced by the increase in research on the benefits of mindfulness in schools, and see mindfulness as a foundation for flourishing (Cherkowski et al., 2018). We have found that teachers have benefited from our inclusion of mindfulness practices in our work with them to encourage and sustain conditions for flourishing in schools.

Compassion

Compassion can be described as noticing and wanting to act to alleviate the pain and suffering of fellow persons. Compassion may also be seen as the mindful awareness of the interconnectedness of our lives and the impact that our actions and thoughts have on one another. At its deepest level, compassion evokes a desire to act in a generous way towards all humans in an effort to alleviate physical, emotional, psychological, and spiritual suffering. Practicing compassion is not only an act of service towards others; the practice has been found to increase personal feelings of happiness (Lyubomirsky, 2006) and reduce symptoms of depressions (Williams, Teasdale, Segal, & Kabat-Zinn, 2007). Compassionate school environments provide opportunities for community members to give and receive of the benefits of compassion.

Researchers on compassion indicate that compassion responses in the workplace can increase affective commitment and positive emotions at work (Lillius, Worline, Dutton & Frost, 2008), are linked to high-quality connections at work (Lillius, Worline, Dutton & Frost, 2011), and can create a virtuous cycle in the workplace (Dutton & Heaphy, 2003). Researchers have found that where organizations support and encourage individual expressions of compassion, capacities are built for collectively noticing, feeling, and responding to pain (Dutton, Worline, Frost & Lillius, 2006; Frost, Dutton, Worline & Wilson, 2000). These findings are relevant for the work of teachers, and we share Wheatley's (2005) assertion that "as leaders, as neighbours, as colleagues, it is time to turn to one another, to engage in the intentional search for human goodness"(p. 57). Teachers, and other school leaders, are essential links in the chain of emotional wellbeing, and the search for human goodness in the school organization. Compassion is important for a healthy organization. As we think about the importance of compassion in building and sustaining relationships with our community members in schools, we can see how practicing and hosting compassion is critical to nurturing an environment where we all thrive.

We know the reality in schools and are aware that schools are often not the easiest places to show compassion. This is especially so as we struggle to work with challenging colleagues and teach students with complex learning challenges. Mindfulness training can be a helpful tool for practicing how to access and act from places of kindness, generosity, and trust, even when we don't always feel that we may want to. As with positive psychology, the rapidly-growing research on mindfulness through use of meditation, yoga, mindful journaling, and various other forms of spiritual disciplines and reflective practice designed to calm to mind, still the body, and open the heart, shows the benefits of engaging in moments of mindfulness at work.

Shifting Ground

Here we offer you an opportunity to try out a mindful practice for cultivating compassion. After you try this activity, you may want to reflect on your **Living Map** about your experience (i.e., what you noticed, what sensations, thoughts, and feelings came up as you carried out the practice, how you feel during and after the practice).

- Take a mindful moment to sit quietly and comfortably.
- Place your hands comfortably on your knees or folded gently in your lap.
- Breathe in and out gently through your nose, paying attention to how the breath feels as it enters and leaves your nostrils.
- Bring to mind and heart a student, colleague, family member, or friend toward whom you wish to extend compassion.
- On your in-breath, can you imagine that person as completely fulfilled and full of love?
- On your out-breath, can you send thoughts of love, care, peace, and happiness to that person?
- Continue to do this for several breaths.
- Now bring your attention to yourself.
- On your in-breath, can you imagine yourself as completely fulfilled and full of love?
- On your out-breath, can you send thoughts of love, care, peace and happiness to yourself?
- Continue to do this for several breaths.

Notice how you feel when you are done your practice. How was this experience for you? You may want to reflect on your **Living Map** about how/if it would be useful to incorporate mindfulness practices, such as this compassion cultivation practice, as part of growing your own flourishing.

Trust

Trust is the second professional virtue that contributes to the flourishing in schools model. Trust has long been researched in educational leadership, and findings show that increased trust links to an improved learning climate in the school (Bryk & Schneider, 2002, Tschannen-Moran, 2004). In our own research, we see the development of trust as hosting or mediating between teachers, leaders, and their learning communities. With colleagues, Keith has written extensively about the role of trust in schools from the perspective of principals and their trust-brokering roles (Kutsyuruba & Walker, 2016, 2015, 2014, 2013; Walker, Noonan, & Kutsyuruba, 2011). Our research has confirmed the essential nature of trust in relationships, its fragility, and the importance of restoring broken trust and remediating betrayal where this has occurred. The stewardship of trusting relationships is critical to the functioning of goodwill within a school setting (Tschannen-Moran, 2004).

According to those we've worked with in schools, a flourishing school is one in which teachers and students engage together to take risks in their learning, innovate in their teaching, and "open their doors to the outside world." Our educator colleagues have shared with us their belief that creating a safe climate for teachers and students to make mistakes is essential to a sense of flourishing. As we've interacted with teachers, trust has been a recurring thread in the responses around what kind of climate might promote a sense of flourishing in schools. One participant described a related perspective:

> The first thing I usually notice about a flourishing school is the relaxed and comfortable way that the staff members interact with each other. It is a comfortable environment where jokes are common and taken in a positive manner. It is a place where risks are taken safely and without fear of personal criticism. When I see this kind of trust utilized by the staff, where they push each other outside of their comfort zones by engaging in research-supported practices, then I believe the school is flourishing.

We have heard from principals about the important work of creating a climate of learning where students and teachers felt safe to experiment and explore alternate ways of teaching and learning. Moreover, creating this safe place for teacher learning was an important aspect of helping teachers to see the possibilities for innovating in their work. As one principal told us, she believed "a culture exists here which allows for risk taking and confidence building. People are innovative and open to trying different things."

Part of what has been shared in the stories we've heard from school principals is that the work of creating trust in schools reflects back on them in ways that gifts them with a deeper sense of meaning in their own work (Cherkowski & Walker, 2016). As captured by much of the current research on trust, creating trust and being trustworthy is not only good for ensuring the work of the school happens in an effective way, but it was also described as a positive and enriching feeling for the person doing the work of building trust. This sense of trust creates a stronger sense of passion in the leader for their own educative work. This is a virtuous cycle that develops in the work lives of principals and other teachers.

Hope

The third virtue featured in the flourishing in schools model is hope. Peter Senge and colleagues (2008) wrote that leadership is "ultimately about shaping futures that we truly desire, as opposed to trying as best we can to cope with circumstances we believe are beyond our control" (p. 372). We see that hope is about recognizing that there is a desired future, and knowing that we can play a role in creating, with others, a new reality that better aligns with who we hope to be as teachers, and as humans. Research shows that this sense of warranted hope about the future is connected to more positive physical, emotional, and mental wellbeing, and that this hope can be cultivated with intentional and ongoing practice.

We think that teachers are important actors in awakening hope, and other positive emotions, in themselves and in the community. As teachers purvey hope they contribute to building with others a common desired future, and this, we think, is at the heart of flourishing as a new school-improvement model. We see that being mindful about the power of our current state helps us to shape and ready ourselves for our preferred futures. We see that by finding a sense of warranted hope we are able to prophetically and morally imagine ourselves, and others, experiencing the positive states we aspire for. As we have found, school communities are sites for flourishing, so for these places and spaces we need to be "constantly and coherently thinking about the future, the Ends, the greater good, the best interests, and larger purposes of each activity taking place in the learning community" (Walker, 2006, p. 555). In other words, the higher good of wellbeing is for the common good.

From much of the writing we have read on leadership, we think that flourishing takes place when leaders (and we suggest everyone in leaderful schools) "uplift our spirits and restore our belief in the future" (Kouzes & Posner, 1993, p. 218). They said, "leaders must keep hope alive"(p. 218) and "arouse optimistic feelings and enable their constituents to hold positive thoughts about the possibilities of success" (p. 221). In addition, each person in the learning community needs to be encouraged to possess adaptive confidence in both themselves and other members of the community (the continuous work of moving individual efficacy towards collective efficacy). Practicing this kind of adaptive and resilient confidence means that "we are willing to enter uncertain situations because we have a higher purpose and we are confident that we can learn and adapt as we move forward" (Quinn, 2004, p. 148). Engaging to co-construct reality in a way that fosters hope and resilience through compassion and building trust is not confined to those with formal leadership titles. Indeed, flourishing communities are dependent on formal and informal leaders recognizing, owning, and acting from a place of adaptive confidence to co-create a desired future that reflects their shared goals and higher purposes.

In the following **Shifting Ground** activity, we provide an opportunity for you to reflect on the best part of this past year, and to notice ways that you can encourage yourself toward ongoing improvement, guided by the virtues of compassion, hope, and trust. This activity was shared with us by a principal in one of our research projects who had teachers engage together in a letter writing experience as a way of wrapping up each year on a positive, hopeful, and appreciative note. He then shared the letters back with them at the beginning of the next year as a way of starting off as a group, guided by their individual and collective sense of hope, trust, and compassion as they think about how to live out their individual and shared dreams and values.

Shifting Ground: Legacy Letter to Self/Community

One example of fostering hope is entailed in the act of writing letters to ourselves, and to our communities, about the future we desire to create with each other. This can serve as an intentional reflection as we remember, write about, and share with others, the best of what we know about our current practice and our dreams for building on that to work towards our desired future. Aligned with the research on increasing happiness and wellbeing, the practice that we now call **Legacy Letters** includes a reflection on an appreciative inquiry approach and notion of agency; we ask you to think about what you did to contribute to what went well. Answer the questions below in as much detail as you can, and then write yourself a letter that you could open at a later time in the year (perhaps at the beginning of the following year). This is an especially powerful practice when done in community:

- What were the highlights for this year?
- How did you engage to cultivate or enrich these highlights?
- What will you continue to do to encourage more of these highlights?
- What will you stop doing to leave more room for highlights in your practice ?
- Imagine you have the power to shape the future. Paint a picture of the future (in words or drawings) that captures the energy, passion, engagement, and hopefulness you desire.
- What is a story about you, as an educator, that you hope to always remember, because it fills your heart when you think of it?

Nurturing Flourishing through Developing your Living Theory

With the growing trend in researching happiness and wellbeing, there is an abundance of theory available to you that can offer conceptual and practical grounding as you build your living theory of flourishing. From an inquiry stance, we also know that there are many different disciplines from which we can draw to build a robust living theory of flourishing. We offer examples of two theories that we use to nurture our own sense of flourishing in our work. One of these theories is from positive psychology, the theory of flow (Csikszentmihalyi, 1997). The other is from philosophy, and is a human-capability theory of development (Nussbaum, 2011).

Nurturing Flourishing through the Theory of Flow

We've long been drawn to the theory of flow, which may be one of the most explicit formulations about activity and subjective wellbeing; understood as the state of mind achieved when the task or challenge is matched by the person's skill level, the activity is seen as pleasurable (Csikszentmihalyi, 1997). Diener (1984) wrote that, "When a person is involved in an activity that demands intense concentration and in which the person's skills and the challenge of the task are roughly equal, a pleasurable flow experience will result" (p. 42). This state of mind that has been described as a deep engagement in the present moment, where the individual is completely absorbed in the activity to the point where time seems to stand still and a deeper, crisper level of consciousness seems to be at work. In these moments, the individual is completely engaged, totally immersed in the activity, fully concentrating and unaware of herself. During these moments, the individual is feeling challenged and stretched in her abilities; she feels efficacious and strong.

In a state of flow, we see how teachers might experience deep levels of engagement, passion, and joy, all of which produce positive feelings in and through their work. From Fredrickson's (2008) research on positive emotions, and her broaden and build theory, we know that experiencing positive feelings in one area of work can open up possibilities for positive experiences in other areas of work and life. We see that this translates to the creative activity of making, and then continuing to engage in building and making your **Living Map** as a personal reflection activity. As you engage in positive reflections on your work, you may find that your creative abilities broaden and you build on what you already know to create and make a map that engages you, interests you, and draws you into a creative experience where you find that moment of flow.

According to Csikszentmihalyi (1997), these states of engagement characterize what it means to live a good and happy life. While the idea of flow can feel elusive, we have often experienced this in our work. For example, Sabre experiences a great sense of happiness and pleasure when she writes. She can lose herself in her writing, aiming to sit down and work for ten or so minutes, only to look up at the clock and see that several hours have flown by. She uses this activity as a positive-energy builder, and tries to find time to write as often as she can throughout the week. She writes for the fun of writing, and then finds that she might have something to offer for a publication. Although she appreciates the opportunity to publish her writing, what she seeks through her time at the computer is not the end product of an article or a book chapter; the activity of writing itself engages her in a sense of flow. She returns to the writing over and over again to experience the positive benefits of this state of engagement. As a simple, and relatable, second example, have you ever picked up a novel and had a hard time putting it down, or engaged in a conversation where time flew by without notice? In our work with teachers, we heard many stories describing how they have noticed what we have been calling flow; a state where you challenge and stretch yourself in enjoyable and non-time-constrained ways that have meaning for you. As another example, one of our school principals described a sense of wellbeing as he noticed what felt good and where he saw room for stretching and growing (Cherkowski & Walker, 2016):

> I believe I work in a flourishing school. It is not a perfect school by any stretch, but every day I see people who are positive and passionate about what they do. They get down and frustrated like anybody, but they are masters at shaking it off because at the end of the day they love what they do ... And there is definitely a culture of fun and sense of humour that supports the flourishing that takes place.

The key to finding moments of flow is learning how to balance current skill sets with the challenge of stretching these skills.

Nurturing Flourishing through a Philosophical Perspective

Returning to our guiding intention, what if the primary role of teachers is to learn how to thrive, and, in so doing, continually co-explore and enthusiastically facilitate all means by which everyone in their learning communities flourishes most of the time? In order to explore and facilitate the means by which everyone in our learning communities can flourish, it is helpful to deepen our thinking about what others have written concerning what it means to flourish. We can look all the way back to the Greek philosophers, such as Plato and Aristotle, and see their seminal reflections on what it meant to live a good life. For example, Aristotle's concept of eudaimonia remains an influential construct for those interested in exploring this idea of living a good life. Essentially, eudaimonia occurs as we gain a sense that we are fulfilling or realizing our true nature – attaining goals throughout our chosen life. For teachers, this could mean that a eudaimonic experience occurs when we are fully engaged in our work; when we are able to express a true sense of self-alignment with our higher purpose in teaching, and when we have a sense of autonomy in how we attain these ends. These experiences can often lead to a sense of feeling alive and authentic in our work.

Through our own inquiry into our living theory of flourishing, we know that a sense of self-improvement and the development of our own practices is only one part of the equation for what it means to flourish. Remembering the reciprocal nature of flourishing, and that we are social creatures, we understand that flourishing is tied to relationships and our abilities to connect and make a difference with each other. Our thriving is often connected to others, and their thriving can be as important as our own. From a philosophical perspective, some who write and research about flourishing suggest that flourishing is about virtuous living, and is the desired end toward which we strive as we aim to live good lives (Nussbaum, 1994). From these perspectives, an inquiry into flourishing includes a sense of attending to the higher purpose of contributing to the enriching of our common humanity. In the following **Heart Print** moment, we invite you to take a few moments to reflect on how flourishing might mean cultivating habits for contributing to the public good through deep engagement and an awareness of self and human potential.

Heart Print

Martha Nussbaum (2011) is a philosopher who listed ten central capabilities that can be understood as benchmark thresholds for all members of the learning community to be at least minimally thriving. We have used this list to reflect on what it might mean to have a more holistic understanding of establishing conditions in schools for all to flourish:

- living a normal life span;
- having good health;
- being able to move freely from place to place;
- being able to use senses (to imagine, think, and reason);
- being able to have attachments (to love and be loved);
- being able to form conceptions of good and engage in critical reflection;
- being able to affiliate with others and engage in respectful social activities;
- living with concern and respect for the world of nature;
- being able to laugh, play, and enjoy; and
- being able to have some control over one's environment (political and material).

> While this paraphrased list may seem basic, we contended that these capabilities can provide good benchmarks for our shift in thinking about understanding schools as vehicles for the positive development of human capabilities (Cherkowski & Walker, 2014, p. 34).

As you read this list, reflect on ways that you experience at least a minimum level of attainment for each of these threshold capabilities in your work as an educator. How do you provide opportunities for students, and others in the community, to experience attainment in these various capabilities in your classroom, and in the school? What does it mean to you to engage in teaching from a human development perspective?

Nurturing Flourishing through Ongoing Creation of your Living Map

We encourage you to engage in documenting your learning journey on your **Living Map** as often as you can, and in whatever ways make sense to you. Perhaps you are moved to create a visual representation of these thresholds on your map, or to establish a structure or routine for reflecting regularly on these capabilities throughout a day, month, or year. We hope the map provides a space for engaging in whatever way you feel best to ignite, inspire, inquire into, and document your learning as you make your way on this journey.

As you engage with this book to construct your **Living Map**, we hope you begin to notice moments of flow, compassion, hope-building, trust, adaptive community, leaderful mindsets, and other nuanced elements entailed in the Flourishing in Schools Model in your work. As you notice, reflect on, and document these moments, you will begin to notice your living theory of flourishing emerging. In this chapter we offered descriptions and examples from the theories and practices from various disciplines, such as positive psychology, positive organizational scholarship, and philosophy that have influenced how we are forming our living theory of flourishing. We hope this gives you a starting point for initial learning and encourage you to spend time reading and learning about your wellbeing, developing a knowledge base that can support and nurture your ongoing pursuit of flourishing.

We also encourage you to share your growing understandings about the importance of wellbeing with your community of trusted colleagues. We think this will likely result in you experiencing a deepened sense of engagement and commitment to supporting your own and others' inquiries. As we will share in the next chapter, building a community within which you can all grow and thrive is an important aspect of sustaining your sense of flourishing.

Chapter Six

Sustaining Through Growing Community

Teachers are social creatures who need and want social attachments; it is part of what it means to participate in being fully human. We want to belong to a group (not just any old group) with whom we can be authentic, act on purpose, and be of service. We want to belong to a group with whom we can derive meaning; meaning in and for our work, and, hopefully, for our lives in general. We acknowledge that our lives "at work" are only partly about work. The work of a teacher is a large part of life, and is entangled (both comfortably or uncomfortably) with who we feel called to be. We want to know that what we do matters; that we are seen and valued, and that we are doing our part to contribute to making these places called "schools" better places for all those who form the learning community. As researchers, teachers, and as people who live in community with others, we have shaped our work and life to be, to do, and to dare; we each seek meaning and purpose in our work-lives and our commitments.

Researchers in various disciplines, such as psychology, business, and the health care fields, show us that the quantity and quality of our relationships connect to how happy and satisfied we feel in our lives, and that our quality of physical health increases with our quality of social networks. The importance of positive social relationships to our overall wellbeing cannot be overstated. Throughout this book, we provide you with opportunities to grow your learning about your self. We've done this with the intention that learning about one's self happens most powerfully in relation to others; those with whom we/you work and live. There is a reciprocity dynamic that operates—when we grow and thrive then others around us seem to do the same, and vice versa. Growing our awareness of who we are and who we intend to become is part and parcel of what it means to grow as humans and teachers in a professional community (Cherkowski et al., 2018).

Consistent with our message so far, we suggest that shifting toward flourishing can happen as an individual and collective aspiration for cultivating conditions at work that promote and nurture opportunities for wellbeing. From research in positive psychology and positive organizational studies we know that an important component of wellbeing happens through positive relationships with others. From our research with teachers, we know that those who claim a sense of flourishing in their work enjoy opportunities for connecting with their colleagues through collaboration and through social times. These relationships are sites for learning and growth as we engage with—and feed off—each other to build and improve our teaching, learning, and living together. These relationships are also essential for sustaining us when we need support, care, reassurance, and rest. While we have described the importance of supporting and encouraging teachers to attend to their self-care at work, we want to emphasize the importance of the relational component to sustain our work, and each other, as we shift toward a mindset of flourishing in and through our work.

The essence of a Flourishing Learning Community (FLC) is belonging to a group with whom we can derive meaning for our work, and, hopefully, for our lives. We want to know that what we do matters. We want to know that we are seen and valued, and that we are contributing to making a difference and helping to make our world a better place. There are four fundamental human longings, expressed in many ways: security (safety and subsistence), significance (meaning), community (belonging), and transcendence (purpose). We yearn and thirst for these and their regular renewal because our nature as persons demands our attention to them. Of course there are many short-term and substitute provisions for these human desires. Sometimes these are called "empty calories for the soul." Despite these ineffectual efforts, there are sustainable ways and means that we can continually strive to be fulfilled in these matters of the heart and humanness. As social and interdependent beings, community is crucial for striving to satisfy and retain the prospect that provides for these longings.

Flourishing learning communities recognize the roles of purpose, belonging, meaning-making, and support in the deepening of connections to school environments and the infinite value of collegial support as teachers seek to sustain their commitment to the profession of teaching. In our research, teachers indicated to us that flourishing environments are ones hosted with a strong sense of togetherness, being on purpose, and personal safety within an atmosphere where playfulness, excitement, and joy all play a strong role in helping them work well together toward improving their students' learning experiences.

This chapter is dedicated to reminding you to recognize that developing your capacity to grow and develop your commitment to your work is a collective phenomenon involving the whole educational community, rather than merely an obligation expected of individual teachers (Jo, 2014). Building the necessary relationships for community takes time, energy, and ongoing inquiry and investment. As we described, positive relationships are a key element of fostering and sustaining wellbeing; they improve our sense of resiliency, our ability to adapt and grow in the face of our constantly changing dynamics of life. They serve as sustainers as we face the inevitable challenges and suffering that are part of human life; they add a richness to the riding out of the challenges, as well as celebrate the triumphs in our work and life (Born, 2014; Block, 2008; Seligman, 2011). Here, we offer theory and practice that you can use to reflect on what it means for you to grow and thrive within a FLC.

Of course, the concept of community has been well-researched in education, framed within perspectives of ethics, professionalism, inquiry, and inclusion (Furman, 2004; Starratt, 2012, 2003; Louis & Marks, 1998; Wenger, 1998). We often build community in schools because we are drawn to work and live together in ways that help us to make deeper meaning of our lives (Block, 2009; Rifkin, 2009; Vanier, 2003). Experiencing a sense of belonging to an authentic community can be transformational for the educator, and we've relied on Scott Peck's (1990) writing to explain the nature of community building as a spiritual journey of transformation. This building up, or edifying community work, requires courage, persistence, patience, and self-awareness, and perhaps the perspective that "the key to community is the acceptance - in fact, the celebration - of our individual and cultural differences. Such acceptance and celebration—which resolves the problem of pluralism and which can occur only after we learn how to become empty—is also the key to world peace" (Peck, 1990, p. 187). The experience of community can be described as a connection with spirituality, deep humanness and notions of peace, appreciation, valuing and receiving gifts of love and attention from each other (Vanier, 2003). For Jean Vanier, "peace flows from a communion of hearts in which we discover that we are truly brothers and sisters belonging to a common humanity" (p. 44). Others have described the connection between serving others in community: "true abiding happiness cannot exist while others suffer, and comes only from serving others, living in harmony with nature, and realizing our innate wisdom and the true and brilliant nature of our own mind"(Scharmer & Kaufer, 2013, p. 251). From our conversations with teachers, we know that belonging to an authentic community can be personally and professionally transformative. As has been described by others who write about the power and promise of community, authentic community can often be recognized as a felt experience of inclusion, openness, vulnerability, listening to others, and an enabling of gracious conflict (Block, 2009; Peck, 1990; Vanier, 2003).

We have identified some principles and attributes that underlie successful development and effective extension of learning communities, such as deep respect for each other and a sense of respectful dialogue, collective responsibility, appreciation of diversity where the school is seen as a living system of difference, and a problem-solving orientation where people are encouraged at every juncture to remain flexible, adapt, habituate agility, and tolerate ambiguity and uncertainty in order to foster extensive experimentation (with both failed efforts and successful innovation). We see the potential of FLCs for creating meaningful learning experiences within a just and democratic school organization. We see how shifting our focus toward both a positive organizational framework and a human capability perspective may provide new ways of thinking about the potential of re-claiming a stronger sense of community within the work of teaching. However, we are mindful that a real sense of community requires hard work and skills to move through the various trials and tribulations experienced as groups of individuals learn to value each other and work together toward a common goal.

In our interactions with teachers, they have described the rewarding feelings of working hard together through difficult times. We've heard them share their stories of the positive impact on their work brought about by celebrating the school's successes, and also caring for each other in difficult times. The kinds of connections developed among teachers as they have engaged in the challenging work of building their sense of efficacy and commitment has lead to feelings of wellbeing and resilience capabilities (Day, Sammons, Stobart, Kingston & Gu, 2007). In our conversations, we have come across many stories of flourishing, and gained insights related into the adaptive capacities of flourishing learning communities and their educator-leaders (i.e., in roles, approaches) who have sought to meet challenges and diverse needs and succeeded in doing so (Cherkowski, Hanson & Walker, 2018; Roset, Walker & Cherkowski, 2016, 2016a, 2016b; Roset, Walker, Cherkowski & Wilson, 2017).

Flourishing Learning Communities

We would say that effective schools are characterized as communities of learners where, as Mitchell and Sackney (2009) stated, "real, joyful, human learning is at the centre of educational activity" (p. 2). If we think of schools as living systems that embrace their humanity to become life-enhancing rather than life-destroying, then one way to understand learning communities is as living systems; vibrant and growing communities of learners (Capra, 2004; Mitchell & Sackney, 2009). Where schools are organized around the principles of living systems, the work to increase capacities results in synergy for new skills and knowledge, enhanced and focused resources, and focused commitments (Mitchell & Sackney, 2009, p. 172). Conceptualising schools as flourishing learning communities means organizing in ways that honour, value and uphold a sense of belonging, compassion for all, loyalty, trust, mutual attachments, hopefulness, and shared concerns, as well as opportunities for play, joy, and purpose as lived expressions of the work of teaching and living well together. It seems to us that such communities of learners are typified by their capacity to foster mutual cooperation, emotional support, and personal growth, and to produce a synergy of effort to improve learning for all. We have suggested that reframing and reculturing of schools as true communities of flourishing learners forms the foundations for the building of the personal cognitive, psychological, emotional, and physical resources that transform people for the better, enabling them to thrive.

We have written about how schools are often faced with the challenge of balancing Tonnies' (1957 in Sergiovanni, 1994) concepts of *gemeinschaft* and *gesellschaft.* In the "system world" of *gesellschaft*, scientific rationality, technology, and the market economy are the motivating forces (Cherkowski & Walker, 2014). In this view, we relate to each other because we see some goal or benefit from the relationship; the emphasis is on the "I," and community values are replaced by contractual relationships, with rational-technical sets of expectations, pressures, and accountabilities. Connecting this back to our discussion of creativity, we might say that this is a left-brain view of the organization. In the "life-world" of *gemeinschaft*, natural, generative, and sustainable relationships are the motivating forces. Persons relate to each other because of intrinsic meaning and transformative significance. The focus is on the "we." We might say that this is a right-brain view of the organization, where synergy, creativity, relationships, emotions, intuition, and other relational capacities provide the foundation for connecting with others. While we know that it is unreasonable to assume that organizations are either one of these ways or the other, we think that we can foster more conditions for *gemeinschaft*, where vitality, zest, and thriving are much more likely to exist. In such conditions we intentionally organize more for wholeness, connection, and long-term wellbeing for individuals and the collective. Ideally, organizations, like persons, function with an optimal level of efficiency, analysis, and rationality balanced with empathy, intuitive working, creativity, zest, and play (*gemeinschaft* and *gesellschaft).* We proffer that this is a wholeness-infused view of life and work.

Creating Conditions to Flourish Together in Schools

We've touched on several facets of how flourishing might be seen in the context of school communities. We have offered another conceptual model of schools as sites of human flourishing, grounded in notions of learning community theory, positive theories of wellbeing, collective compassion, and attention to hopefulness for the future. We don't wish to provide models that we think you should merely adopt or follow; rather, we provide these as provocations, as prompts that you may choose to use to reflect on and build your own thinking about engaging in learning toward flourishing for your self and your school. This visual representation of the flourishing metaphor was previously shared in a journal article (Cherkowski & Walker, 2013) and shows the connections between various elements of what we propose as a new way of thinking about school improvement—the *Flourishing Learning Community.* The model is conceptualized as a recursive spiral, or life cycle, of *Flourishing Theories* (antecedent theories, concepts of adult development, and current state-of-the-art practices of school improvement) and *Flourishing Practices* (noticing, inspiring/multiplying, sustaining) that can influence and shape *Flourishing Schools*. The spiraling life cycle of this model is underpinned by theories of adult learning and development where attaining levels of self-actualization, or higher levels of consciousness, is the ultimate human aspiration (Kegan, 1994; Maslow, 1943; Mezirow, 1991)

This model was an initial representation of our understandings, during the early months of our research on flourishing in schools (in the Fall of 2011), of what it could mean to establish a new way of thinking about school improvement. We initially sketched out this model on a napkin or serviette during a shared meal at an academic conference. We remember our excitement as the model took shape through our sharing of ideas, and as we sketched them in a way that made sense to us. As our own energy and interest grew, through our shared napkin-creation conversation, we decided to present this model during our session at this conference. We were excited by the interest and encouragement from our educational research colleagues in supporting the need for developing a positive, appreciative and human development model of school improvement.

The model is grounded in the principle of abundance, and of unlimited potential. We see this shift in mindset from deficiency to unlimited potential as providing new lenses for viewing learning communities as school organizations. Finally, the shadow side of this model is acknowledged, with concepts of fear, systemic barriers, and toxic contributors included in the collection of potential negative detractors located beside the central construct of the model—*Flourishing Schools* (Figure 6.1).

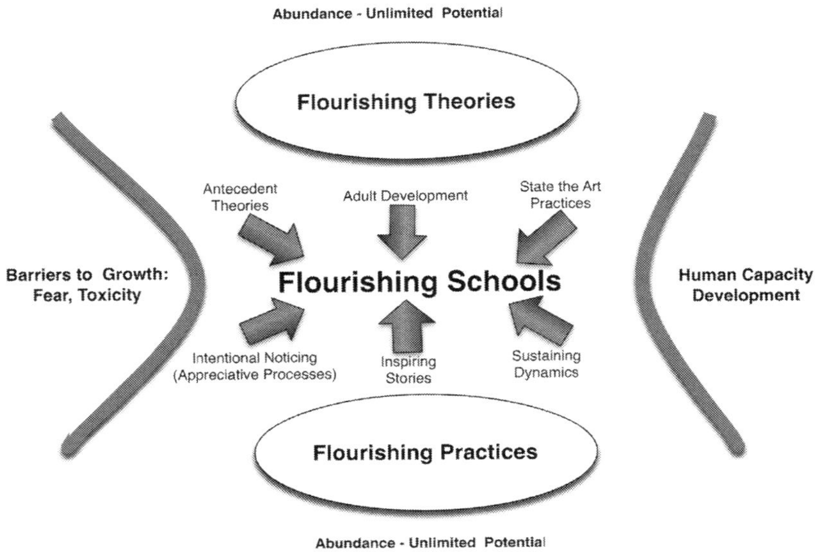

Figure 6.1. Conceptualizing Flourishing Learning Communities

Qualities of a Flourishing Learning Community

We invite you to take some time to work through the various elements of the model, and to reflect on how you see these fitting with your own ideas about what it might mean to create conditions in your school for flourishing—along with your colleagues, students and all others in the learning community. We encourage you to take some time to jot down your reflections on your **Living Map**: what it might mean for you to bring to life the elements that we represent in the figure above? We also encourage you to share your ideas with others in a fashion that will grow and deepen your community as you do the work of flourishing together. In this next section we describe two aspects we've noticed as important for fostering, nurturing, and sustaining flourishing in learning communities in schools: shared leadership and collaborative relationships.

Shared leadership

As you will have picked up by now, we believe that students (and teachers) do their best learning in supportive, compassionate, and caring environments. Through this chapter, we have emphasized the importance of developing new ways of thinking about educational communities from a positive perspective. If a community of learners is framed as a setting or space where people congregate to flourish together, then teachers are the leaders in the building of these dynamic communities. Like the word "relationship," leadership describes the chemistry of community connections between and among people, rather than something that is inherent within the person (or persons) themselves. In other words, you aren't a relationship or a leadership; leadership and relationships reside in the spaces, practices, and hyphens between and among people (i.e., leaders-followers). An excellent relationship speaks to the quality of connections between two or more persons; similarly, leadership speaks to the intentional effort of connected persons to strive towards creating more flourishing within a setting, and within the members of the community. We might even say that leadership is a condition that affords connections among people. Flourishing people will naturally, out of their own thriving, influence others to flourish. What emerges from this way of framing learning communities is a vision that sees everyone as an educator, every member as a leader, and all participants as learners. You'll recall our earlier mention of "leaderful" flourishing learning communities. We'll address this further in our Epilogue.

It is our contention that teachers are benefited when they understand and assume their role as animators and hosts within leaderful, resilient, reciprocal, and learningful settings (Cherkowski & Walker, 2013). Raelin (2003) offered the view that leaderful and adaptive learning communities will have concurrent, collective, collaborative, and compassionate features. He said that in leaderful practice, followership and leadership are in essence part of the same process "... [where] leaders and followers are the interchangeable parts in the conduct of leadership"(p. 36) for the accomplishment of some greater and higher common purpose (we suggest this is fostering flourishing).

Collaborative Relationships as Sites of Learning to Flourish

Building and sustaining collaborative relationships through shared leadership and reflection on teaching and learning, co-constructions of cultures through sharing values and goals, and a strong desire for teachers to work collaboratively to improve learning experiences for all students, are all elements of collaborative relationships that are necessary conditions for learning communities in schools. For teachers, these opportunities can also be moments to grow themselves, personally and professionally, and to engage in collaborations. In part, this is what it means to cultivate one's self through teaching. Appropriately, much of the research on collaboration focuses on improved professional learning and student achievement (Lieberman & Mace, 2010; Stoll & Louis, 2007). From a flourishing perspective, we see that collaboration also provides an opportunity to create meaningful relationships and a sense of individual and collective achievement at work. This sense of wellbeing at work empowers teachers to build climates of professional learning where educators engage regularly in reflective dialogue with each other about what is working well and how to continuously enrich the learning experiences they provide for their students (Cherkowski et al., 2018). Attending to wellbeing is important, although we have contended that it is often overlooked as a vital aspect of professional learning communities. We have found that the realities of teachers' work worlds often seem to offer more obstacles than opportunities for creating the conditions for sustainable learning communities (Brown & Cherkowski, 2011; Cherkowski, 2012, 2016; Cherkowski & Ragoonaden, 2017). Despite teachers' espoused desires for greater collaboration, it is rarely achieved in schools due to the lack of time, intense workload, and structures that promote isolation and hierarchical power arrangements (Cherkowski & Schnellert, 2014, 2017). Not surprisingly, these same barriers are the ones we mentioned in the first chapter when describing the contributing factors to teacher burnout. When teachers experience their work as meaningful opportunities to engage with colleagues toward improving their practice, and enjoy the process and benefits of collaboration, they feel a sense of wellbeing. While we continue to hear many stories about the impossibility of meaningful collaboration, such as those listed above, we also have heard many stories from participants in our research on flourishing that describe experiences of the wellbeing that come from working well with others towards that which matters most to them: student success.

Sustaining through Framing our Work in Flourishing Ways

In a hope-giving way, a mentor once told us, "No condition is permanent!" From this we interpret that all parts of our life are constantly changing, the good and the bad, and that we might as well find ways to grow more of what we want when we can, and to lessen our suffering when we can. We appreciate that a deep commitment to service has its cost and tolls, but where we can exercise our choice to alleviate pain, suffering, and ill-effect, we should pursue these means.

As we've journeyed along in our research, fellow teachers have shared with us their definitive understanding of learning to find ways to create positive conditions in their work. Where and when they could do so, they have promoted and encouraged laughter, play, and having fun with colleagues and other members of the learning community. As well, they have sought to establish systems of support, care, hope, and belonging as essential aspects of how they set about their flourishing, amidst the challenges, complexities, and constantly changing environments in their schools and communities. Here is the wonderful thing we have learned: exercising my sense of humour, laughing out loud, being playful, and simply having fun, as well as responding with care, kindness, and concern, to my colleagues and students, are ALL within my realm of unpreventable control. In other words, I can BE cheerful or I can rain on other people's parades. I can build myself and others up to feel well. So much of this has to do with moment-by-moment choices I make. Indeed, one participant told us, "You couldn't ask for a better place to work, or a better group of people to work with. I mean it's fun, it's engaging for us, it's engaging for the kids." This sounds good, doesn't it?

Given the evidence from psychology and neuroscience about the importance of positive emotion for engagement, perseverance, and innovation in learning, it would seem essential that we begin to take seriously the idea of playfulness, joy, lightness, and laughter in the work of teaching and leading schools. We have suggested that there ought to be a shift in the balance of our attention toward focusing on what is working well and fostering more vitality, joy, compassion, kindness, creativity, and other virtuous behaviours and capabilities. This is a reiteration of our call in the last chapter for paying more attention to the lifeworld of schools (*gemeinschaft*), encouraging more creativity, intuition, play, and zest that can be felt as we engage with others in collaboration toward mutually agreed on desired ends that benefit all in the community. This positive shift to focusing on robust and nourishing aspects of human experience in the context of schooling is vital for improving our efforts to improve education.

Using what we know from research in positive psychology, and from positive change theories such as appreciative inquiry, we assume that if we are able to shift how we think and the ways we tell ourselves stories about our experiences, then we can shift enough of our actual experience to alter how we understand and react to our perceived reality. In this next **Heart Print** moment we offer a series of questions that will prompt you to shift the way you think about learning communities and your role within them. We think these questions might shift an inquiry toward a fresh understanding of how we, as teachers, can focus on developing human capacities, such as compassion, social justice, and democratic processes, as part of our work as educational leaders in our school communities. We suggest that you use your **Living Map** to capture your reflections and document new questions that may come up for you.

Heart Print

Questions can shift the focus of our inquiry. Different and fresh questions can shift us even further in our inquiry. Shifting our questions can provide access to experiences that influence and shape who we are and who we hope to become. We think these questions have potential for focusing our thinking and action in purposeful ways:

- What does it mean to thrive in school?
- How do we relate to each other when we are working at our best?
- What is the purpose and meaning of teaching, learning, and school, in relation to the larger context of what it means to be human?
- How can we create conditions for joy, zest, vitality, and play within our context?

Restorying our schools as communities is crucial for cultivating conditions where teachers more fully and consistently feel a sense of belonging, empathy, and connection in ways that are inextricably linked and interwoven with our responses to these questions (Cherkowski & Walker, 2014). We think there is promise and potential in using positive frameworks to shift our view of schools to explicitly give attention to how we develop and deepen the human capabilities, relationships, and the meanings we share in school communities, in ways that supports growth as human beings within that community. These relationships are an important aspect of growing and sustaining our wellbeing at work. Focusing on the importance of meaningful and rich relationships as an integral part of the work of teaching can provide a starting point for re-storying schools as positive and thriving learning communities. We encourage you to deepen your learning by having a conversation with some colleagues about your emerging ideas and thoughts about the questions and contents of this chapter.

In the next **Shifting Ground** activity we provide a few guidelines that you might want to consider practicing as you engage with trusted and supportive colleagues in conversations about shifting your work, and your school, toward working, learning, and leading together for flourishing.

Shifting Ground: Celebration Circle

Learning to communicate openly and effectively, learning to disagree respectfully, learning to develop work teams and learning to disband teams that are not working, learning to demonstrate compassion and care, learning to draw out passion, fun, and joy in ourselves at work and with those with whom we share our day – these are important tools for growing flourishing learning communities in our classrooms, staffrooms, and across our schools.

Talking circles can be a meaningful way to share in each other's company and to practice deep listening. We spend a large amount of time at our workplaces, and, as we discussed in Chapter Five, we can sometimes struggle in our attempts to "fit in" all we "have to do" in the framework of our 8 hour (or 24 hour) days. To truly experience a celebration circle, we need to let go of the frustrations we can experience when we are asked to listen. We can help support this process with the following protocols for circle speaking.

- Say just enough;
- Speak only from "I" perspective; and
- Listen with an open heart.

You can organize your celebration circle in many different ways. If you are reading this book as part of a group, each member might bring a key reflection from the activities or their reading, including (for example) their map to share with the other group members. If you are reading this book alone, invite a group of colleagues to listen to your journey. The object is not to agree with or critique each other; it is simply to reflect on how we can learn more about ourselves by learning about, and from, others. Take some time after the circle process to reflect on what you learned about your self, your community, about the process of celebration circles, as well as your dreams and aspirations for using the practices and reflections that we've shared in this book so far (as well as many others that you already know and use) to grow flourishing learning communities in your school.

≋

Through our research we have grown in our appreciation of the importance of community for fostering and sustaining a sense of flourishing for teachers. In other words, flourishing often happens from, with, and through the ongoing process of developing and sustaining relationships of trust, care, connection and belonging, purpose, and enjoyment. These relationships contribute to building a supportive community for strong teaching and learning, where teachers feel safe to try out new practices and a sense of freedom to shift, grow, and change in their work. This work of teaching-as-community-building takes time, energy, ongoing inquiry, and investments of emotional and structural supports for creating spaces where teachers can regularly connect and work together. These supports for building and growing community for flourishing include common work and break times, opportunities and capacities for ongoing collaboration, administrator support and encouragement, as well as hiring and organizational practices that promote and value relationships and community for fostering and sustaining wellbeing. However, as we reiterate our message throughout this book, we don't think teachers need to, nor should they, wait for others to set the conditions for their wellbeing. Instead, we encourage you to find ways to create conditions for community now. Do so in your current context, in your present teaching configuration, and under your current workplace conditions. Make room for this – even if, to begin with, the space afforded for these initiatives are modest. We encourage you to seek out opportunities to connect with colleagues—wherever they may be—for support, enjoyment, a sense of knowing others and being known, and for feeling that you belong to a group making a difference in the world. As we describe in the next chapter, carving out your learning journey toward flourishing is yours to do, and pursuing wellbeing with others is powerful.

Chapter Seven

The Flourishing Journey for Self and Others

Throughout this book we have sought to develop and draw out this process of creating a **Living Map** of learning about flourishing. As you think about your learning so far, we hope you're becoming aware of how a living theory of flourishing promotes attention to both theory and practice, and to an abundance mindset rather than a deficit-model way of thinking. We hope you are starting to **notice** what makes you flourish and are making time and space to **nurture** this sense of thriving in ways that work for you. We hope that you're on the lookout for others with whom you can share this work, building a community to **sustain** the work of learning to **flourish**.

All of the theory and practice presented so far resonates with our beliefs and convictions that schools are organizations that can be understood as living systems, full of mysteries and wonderful complexities, because they are created, constructed, and enacted through the beautifully-tangled webs of human relationships. We have witnessed the beauty of watching and connecting with teachers who are deeply, even profoundly, implicated in these marvellous, human, learning ecosystems. As we wind down this learning journey about what it means to flourish in your work as teachers, we will take a few moments to describe our thoughts about the importance of a renewed call to teachers to become leaders of leaders, servants of leaders, advocates for flourishing and of flourishing learning communities. This call to leadership (the conditions and practices for dynamic, leaderful, and flourishing schools) is not traditional. We are not offering a lone-hero or lone-ranger approach to managing schools.

You will see no one person riding into a school situation on a white horse with a white hat. Rather, the shared and collaborative leadership that we imagine as necessary for creating conditions where all members of a community can thrive is collective, relational, and deeply influenced by an awareness and understanding of self in relation to the educative work of bringing life to a school community.

In our conversations with teachers and principals, we have learned that leadership for flourishing is predicated on the assumption that every person in the community is important. Important period. Not important because...but important period. This critical assumption ought to be self-evident; something so worth the time and effort required to comprehend and to build relationships of mutual care, trust, and support. This imputation of dignity and worth to all, and the kind of relational leading we are advocating, happens at all levels of the organization, not just by those in formal leadership positions. We are strong, strong, advocates of "every student leadership and followership," "every parent leadership and followership," and "every staff member and teacher leadership and followership." Leadership and followership are not an exclusive club – schools are best when they are "aristocracies of everybody" (our thanks to Benjamin Barber for this phrase) – schools where everybody is a somebody!

This said, we also believe that the formal school leader, the principal, plays an essential role in nurturing, sustaining, and making room for a climate that values and honours relationships as a primary element of the work of bringing life, together with appropriate levels of messiness and order, to a school. From our experience, and the stories we've picked up along the way, we would say that the school principal plays a central role in fostering and sustaining a professional learning climate where teachers can thrive. Starratt (2011) called this role a human-resource-development one and wisely suggested that we need to think about reframing our perspective of what it means to be a principal toward this capacity-building role. We suggest we need to continue to support principals to develop positive leadership capacities for the purpose of growing more flourishing for all in schools. More on this in our next chapter.

We also urge for re-framing leadership as a mindset, or sense of agency, for growing environments of wellbeing for all through building community capacity for all. This means leadership is about building capacity for, by, and with all members of the school—teacher, staff, students, and parents--to participate as active and positive leaders and followers, creating together cultures of caring, trust, and hope. We can all think of ourselves as called to the service of ongoing, personal, professional development—of self and others—as we engage in our work of teaching and learning, with our intended goal being to share among many the opportunities for both leadership and followership in the flourishing learning community.

From our work, and our own experiences, with educational leaders across various educational contexts, we know that while many teachers have personal dispositions and capacities for engaging themselves and others in an ongoing pursuit of thriving in their work, there are others who might benefit from gentle nudging toward engaging in this flourishing mindset through ongoing professional learning and development. This might take the form of appreciative inquiry, the use of social interventions to increase positive emotions at work, finding occasions to develop growth mindsets and other positive traits, the use of mindfulness techniques as tools for stress reduction, conversations about the role of compassion, trust and hope in our lives, and engagement in exercises that consider strengths-based living and leadership (Cherkowski & Walker, 2016).

These descriptions of leaderful mindsets, and examples of initiatives designed to overcome inertia and to foster healthy educational leadership, are open to all members of the community. In these ways (to name only a few), each member of the community can be called to engage more deeply in reflecting on their strengths, talents, temperaments, and gifts as human-capacity developers. Each educator can be challenged to own, and engage deeply in, their own professional autonomy, efficacy, and relatedness as an educator, and to take seriously (as a calling) the role of developing the human capacities of the students and colleagues with whom they work.

Working from a positive leadership approach means coming to an awareness of our values, biases, beliefs, and assumptions, noticing how these are lived out in our work, and making decisions about our ongoing engagement from an appreciative, positive, and growth-promoting way. This is often accomplished using personal inventories and tools that serve as reflective instruments for personal, professional growth. Engaging with others in processes that help us to think together about what is working well, and what changes are needed, can be powerful learning experiences. Because relationships ought to be privileged and take center-stage in flourishing learning communities, these conversations about working as positive leaders for flourishing can, and should, happen on many different occasions: at regular staff meetings, in the staff room during lunch, or during professional development days and sessions. Those who are invested in the work of developing and growing human capacity among all teachers, administrators, and staff will be instrumental, catalytic, and animating purveyors of a sense of synergy of purpose in flourishing learning communities.

We also see the importance for policy-makers to contribute to cultivating flourishing and leaderful schools. For example, we noted how Day et al. (2007) recommended that policy-makers ensure provision for personnel support structures to "address the associations between teachers' wellbeing, and their commitment, self-efficacy and resilience" (p. 238). From positive psychology research, we know about interventions that can increase personal feelings of wellbeing, and so we suggest that starting with teachers (and other school leaders) can be an important step in our understanding about how to support the wellbeing and resilience of all the members of a learning community. Further, teacher education and leadership development programs can become the initial point for conversation about the kinds of practices and habits of mind that support a sense of flourishing, in self and others, in the work of teaching and leading learning in others (Cherkowski & Walker, 2013b).

As the idea of leaderful mindsets in organizations resonates in the school and corporate literatures, and as we better understand the importance of sharing leadership across an organization, these distributive practices will result in the practical dispersing of large amounts of flourishing work in school settings. The work belongs to all the community members. We see that intentional processes of co-designing and co-creating a shared image of a desire future is the only viable path to transforming schools. Scharmer and Kaufer (2013) described this new kind of collective leadership, such as combines the ideas of collaborative learning and leading with knowing self and others, as a shift from 'ego-systems' to 'eco-systems'. They invited people to explore three dimensions: "(1) better relating to *others*; (2) better relating to the *whole* system; and (3) better relating to *oneself*" (p. 16). As we described, Scharmer's (2009) *Theory U* model of leadership for change connects the research on mindfulness and the importance of establishing a collective sense of presence, intention, and purpose as part of a collaborative learning journey toward co-creating a desired future. He suggested that this co-creation happens swiftly as soon as all participants learn to engage with an open heart, an open mind, and an open will. There are several practices, such as deep listening and meditation moments, that can help create the energy needed to tap into this fertile source for inspiring change and transformation.

As we have thought about flourishing schools, we know from our own experiences, and from our conversations with colleague-teachers, that accessing a space of collaborative dialogue can be a generative experience. For example, given time and space, collaboration can become a positive, energy-producing experience as each me mber of the group becomes engaged. Collaboration creates a community where we enjoy each other, support each other, and challenge each other to improve in our practice. Regardless of what you have experienced in the past, the experiences we have described are a very real possibility for any school. We have both experienced and heard from others about moments of deep presence and listening, of a strong and intense sense of connection to each other and to a larger system of connections, and of a creativity and sense of ease about co-creating opportunities for ongoing personal professional growth. To reiterate, We often refer to Margaret Wheatley's argument that in the future, "those organizations who will succeed are those that evoke our greatest human capacities—our need to be in good relationships, and our desire to contribute to something beyond ourselves" (p. 124).

Enhancing Teacher Wellbeing

The main attention of this book has been on teacher wellbeing in the context of schools, and individual and collective flourishing. We wrap up our discussion of teacher wellbeing with an example from research that resonates with the ideas and suggestions we have made so far. Marks (2011) suggested that happiness requires a need to focus on **relationships** and to connect with a wide variety of people (location 463-4722). He proposed that building connections supports and enriches life, and differentiated between thick and thin relationships explaining, "Our thick relationships are our close intimate relationships and our thin ones are our broader circle of friends, relatives work colleagues, neighbours and people we know in our daily lives" (locations 468-71). Both types of relationships are vital for nourishing oneself. Tom Rath's (2006) commendable work on *Vital Friends* provides other approaches to enhancing workplace and personal-space friendships.

Marks' second suggestion was that teachers commit to becoming **physically active**, because this activity is associated with increased wellbeing and with lower rates of depression (location 473-479). Physical activity protects against cognitive decline in later years, and it enhances learning in both teachers and children. Third, Marks advocated **curiosity, awareness, and appreciation** of the world, and to reflect and savour the experiences throughout the day (location 479-484). Paying attention to thoughts, feelings, and sensations enhances our lives, and helps us to choose actions and behaviours that fit with our interests and values. This, too, certainly resonates with the organization of this book and our other suggestions.

Fourth, Marks offers that it is imperative to **keep learning** and to challenge oneself, for it promotes self-confidence, fun, and happiness (location 484-494). When we feel encouraged, or inspired, to learn, we are likely to improve our cognitive and social skills, increase our self-confidence, feel a stronger sense of purpose, and continue to build our skills and competencies. Goal-setting and the process of achieving those goals enhance happiness. The fifth strategy that Marks suggested entails **giving to others,** because to do so increases our happiness and contributes to a sense of meaning in the teacher's life (location 494-500). Being generous and altruistic has positive benefits for teacher wellbeing—and for those in their circles of concern and influence.

In the next **Shifting Ground** moment, we offer practices to reflect on what it might mean for you to commit, or recommit, to habits and mindsets of resilience and wellbeing; ones that enhance your wellness, nudging and shifting your life and work towards increased wellbeing through being well, whole, alive, engaged, on purpose, and having fun in your ongoing pursuit of growing and thriving at work. As we will share below, and as we indicated in our opening chapters, flourishing is a fluid and aspirational destination, and there is not one perfect way of attaining or sustaining this balance for living well. Life is constantly shifting and moving, as it always has and as it always will. Our challenge is to learn to be well in the moment, and to learn how to recognize and ask for more supports to help us move toward wellbeing when we notice that we are leaning too far toward our 'Just Surviving Island' or 'Burnout Island'. Sometimes, reflecting on how others are also experiencing challenges and difficulties can provide the perspective we need to shift into an appreciative or grateful state of mind, heart, and body. We offer an example of an activity we have used with teachers to have them notice what they need for self-care, and to develop strategies to adjust their practices if they find they are leaning too far away from their wellbeing habits, routines, and ways of being.

Shifting Ground: Noticing and Attending to Self-Care

When afforded the opportunity to work with teachers, leaders, or groups of human service professionals, we have offered a simple laminated card (Figure 7.1) to them. We've suggested that self-care is really important, and encouraged them to find ways to commit themselves to this in both principle and practice. We've said that most of us are "educated beyond our obedience!" In other words, we usually know what we ought to do—it is just a matter of prioritizing actually doing it. There are some very simple practices (we've identified six from the resilience and wellbeing literature) that, if habituated in the routines of the teacher's life, will make a positive difference. These are simple but life-giving and refreshing activities. There are many ways to personalize and adapt these research-grounded initiatives, and activities that foster our flourishing are plentiful (so, on the cards, we've provided some other examples). May we challenge you to commit to the principle of self-care for wellbeing and encourage you to incorporate the six simple activities into your life and lifestyle?.

SELF-CARE for EDUCATORS

My work can be overwhelming but it makes a positive difference in the lives of others! It is essential that I take care of my own wellbeing so I can steward my care and skills on behalf of others. My resilience matters!! I've chosen to flourish and find ways to help others do the same. Self-care is a series of daily and conscious and pro-active choices for me.

I WILL DO THESE SIX THINGS EACH DAY

1. I will get enough good sleep
2. I will get enough nutritious food to eat
3. I will get some exercise (i.e., take the stairs)
4. I will express my gratitude, out loud, to another
5. I will take time to pause, to pray, to meditate or to relax
6. I will give something of worth to someone (i.e., hug, kind word)

OTHER RESILIENCE BUILDERS

Share a laugh. Do random smile self-checks. Learn from my mistakes and move on. Vary the work that I do. Do some physical stretching. Focus on what I did well today. Stop twice a day to "tactically" breath, check-in, move ahead. Sing, whistle or tap into some good music. Put away the work I've brought home tonight or on the weekend and instead . . . rest and renew. Talk feelings with a trusted friend. Set small, quick win smart goals. Read a book. Set a limit on the time and energy to optimize a task or project. Envision myself at my best. Do something pleasurable. Treat myself to a compliment (well done!). Complement or encourage a colleague. Recount what I've learned today. Go for coffee with a new friend or colleague. Show authentic interest in another. Recruit help and forego self-sufficiency. Go for a walk to nowhere for 5 minutes (take a break). Name my pain. Let go of hurt – forgive and move on. Decide not to sweat the small stuff. Breathe deeply and calmly as I start in on a tough job. Actively invite and listen to someone's story. Pay something forward or secretly give something of value to another. Decide to be flexible. Take a different route to somewhere. Plan and take a real vacation.

Figure 7.1 Front and Back of Self-Care Card for Educators (Walker, 2017)

Perhaps you'd consider inviting others to join you in this commitment to self-care. Feel free to use this card, or adapt it, or create your own devices for fostering flourishing

In the following **Shifting Ground** moment, we invite you to connect with a colleague, or a friend, or perhaps your partner or a family member. This activity is designed to offer you an experience of presence, listening, and deep connectedness. This activity is called an empathy walk. We learned about it in an open-source course on *Theory U* offered by Otto Scharmer. He uses the empathy walk experience to promote the power of empathy as a connector, and as a way to shift the field of consciousness toward the suffering of others in ways that can increase our own sense of appreciation and gratitude. We have adapted it here for you.

Shifting Ground: Empathy Meeting

Think about someone you think you know quite well. Arrange to have coffee with this person for the purpose of finding out how they are doing, what they are most passionate about right now, what is most worrying them, and so on. Before you meet, write down a list of questions you might ask—and what you think will be the response. Meet that person, and spend at least 30 minutes listening attentively. After your time with this friend, take a moment by yourself to jot down some notes about what you've learned. Then, compare what you learned to what you thought you knew. What do you notice about your feelings about the

experience? What have you learned about your friend and what did the experience evoke in you? How might this activity be useful at work? Add to your **Living Map** any new insights and understandings about what it means to know yourself, to know this other person better, and to recognize that leadership is about engaging with others in the collective pursuit of co-creating a desired future.

≈

Learning From Our Living Map

Margaret Wheatley (2012) suggested that what often keeps change from happening is our relentless need to follow a map that we think is leading us to where we want to be going. She suggested that admitting that we may be lost, and that our old maps may be for a time and place that no longer fits where we want to go, is a step in the right direction of starting to see where we really are and who we really are in a more curious, open, and honest way. Part of developing your **Living Map of Flourishing** has been to let yourself have a creative, emergent, and open experience with what it might mean to flourish; to allow new ideas and new practices to resonate with you as you reflect on your new thoughts, ideas, and aspiration, trusting that where you are headed is where you need to go. And we hope that creating your **Living Map** has also been about finding the space and grace to let go of old maps, dead-end ideas, or ineffectual and disappointing ways that no longer serve you and others. This is an ongoing process, with many twists and turns, with moments of moving forward and moments of moving back. What to keep, what to improve, what to innovate, what to stop and what to start? These are important questions as we design our way toward wellbeing.

One of our last reflection activities is a combined **Heart Print and Shifting Ground** moment. We use the metaphor of a river to encourage you to notice the playfulness of water as a river slips and slopes its way through the many rocks, curves, and crooks along the way. What might it feel like to live out our work in this spirit of lightness and playfulness? To know that nothing is likely ever going to remain the same, and the most fun we can have while we make our way down this winding river is to learn to be well, supported and supportive, and to be as useful as we can to others in encouraging them to learn how to live in a light and open-hearted way? This may seem daunting—even unrealistic—but we know from our social constructionist understandings that we can choose, at any moment, to respond in a variety of ways to any stories, even those that seem unrealistic and unattainable. We can choose to believe that playfulness, openness and light-heartedness, kindness and compassion, are all available responses to each of us, at any time. We also know that we likely have to practice these more appreciative and positive responses over and over again, until they become our preferred habit. Sabre often jokes about how she wishes that living wellbeing and flourishing was as easy as writing about it! However challenging it may be to gain a sense of presence, appreciation, and compassion for self and others as a way of life, we are confident enough in saying that the need for these shifts in our schools is greater than the discomfort of learning new ways of teaching, leading, and being for teachers, students, and all others in the school community.

From that positive stance we invite you to open your mind and heart to experiencing the combined **Heart Print and Shifting Ground** moment, and to take the time to document your learning on your **Living Map**. We also encourage you to connect with others to share all of your learning, and to share your dreams, desires, and passions for shifting toward flourishing. As we have been bold enough to say out loud, both to each other and to our audiences, whether in person or on paper, we believe we are at a special time, when findings in the social and natural sciences are aligning with our long-held wisdom about the imperative of connection, belonging, appreciation, generosity, creativity, intuition, zest, play, and love—among so many other ways we feel the most human and engaged with our self and with others in our lives. We invite you to join with us on this ongoing, learning journey of transforming ourselves and our worlds through positive, appreciative, generative, and love-filled ways and means. Not only does that **Living Map** lead toward flourishing (in schools and in life), but it seems to be, to us at least, an incredibly worthwhile way of spending our time together as teachers who care deeply about positively influencing people. So, find the time to go sit by a river, if there is one nearby, or even find a river on YouTube and spend some quiet time watching and listening to the playfulness of the water. Enjoy the experience and enjoy the reflection time with your Living Map.

Heart Print and Shifting Ground

Find a river. Go there (this could be in your neighborhood or one created virtually, or in your mind's eye). Watch the river with a sense of curiosity and wonder.

How does it move so freely? Notice how full of life the river appears.

How has creating your **Living Map of Flourishing** been like a river?

Have you found yourself floating or being swept along? When have you clung to the banks of the river?

A river is essentially a path; in fact from high above it might be difficult to distinguish between a river or a path or a road. Wheatley (2012) asked, "What is it that streams can teach me about organizations" (p. 17)? She was drawn to water to teach herself about adapting, trusting, letting go and going with a flow. Each flourishing map is unique, each path shifts and changes in unexpected ways. Rivers flow, offering us the metaphor of hope and faith, knowing that as we move purposefully toward what matters most we can divert around the obstacles while continuing on our way. The work of flourishing requires trust in the process, a forward motion, and a sense of faith that

> the outcome is eventually attainable as we continue to move together toward our desired future, shifting and changing our path as necessary.

Seeing your learning journey as a flowing river might offer new insights for how to let yourself 'go with the flow' to experience the richness of the stream. As you think about flourishing, and observe the river, imagine yourself stepping in and then floating. What does it feel like to flow with the river? How does the water feel? How does your skin feel? How does this experience awaken ideas, feelings, and thoughts within you? What do you feel floating within you? Where do you notice you resist floating and are, perhaps, clinging to a rock or to the side of river? These reflection questions are prompts to have you notice, in a deep and present way, what experiences are evoked as you engage with the real or imagined river. You might find some interesting revelations about how you go with the flow, how you resist change, how you embrace the unknown, or how you relish certainty. As with all the activities and practices we've offered in this book, we encourage you to notice without judgment, staying open to what you can learn about the flow of flourishing. Enjoy this reflective moment, and take some time to document your reflections on your map.

Learning to Flourish through Teaching: Our Encouragement to You

Based on our research, and the experience of others, we have said that attending to strengths and positive outlooks, as opposed to a deficit-model of thinking, can increase resilience, vitality, and happiness, and can decrease stress, anxiety, and depression. We see how we can use the findings the science of positive psychology in the service of greater flourishing in school communities and in the lives of teachers. We know that social-emotional learning is linked to increased academic achievement and is recognized as an important element for student development and success in school and in life (Cohen, 2001; Greenberg, Weissberg, Utne & Resnik, 2003). From a positive psychological perspective, increasing or maximizing social-emotional learning is an essential element in establishing habits for lifelong learning, but also for lifelong wellbeing. Moreover, being happy and feeling good are often necessary precursors to meaningful learning and development, so attending to feeling good at school is a necessary step in establishing school climates where children and their teachers can thrive.

There is also a growing awareness that learning is a social process, and that much of what goes on in schools happens in a social context. Students do not learn alone; they learn in collaboration with their peers, their teachers, and with others in their learning community. Attending to emotions and social processes is an essential element in creating positive and caring learning climates where students can thrive. We suggest that teachers also need similar learning climates in order to take risks in their practice, to make mistakes, to open their individual practice to collaborative inquiry, to pursue their passion, to engage in meaningful relationships with their colleagues, and to create moments of play in their work—flourishing learning communities. Knowing that meaningful learning happens when we feel cared for, feel good, and are generally happy (Knoop, 2011), we consider wellbeing to be an integral element of a positive learning climate where students and teachers can flourish. As we continue to live the questions that open us to the complexity of the human spirit, we are awakened to our crucial work of exploring how we best host the professional virtues of compassion, trust, and hope. We sense that developing a personal understanding of flourishing may be central to learning, and central to what it means to become an educator.

What if you were to imagine that your primary role as an educator is to learn how to thrive in your role, and, in so doing, to continually co-explore and enthusiastically facilitate all means by which each person in your learning community flourishes along with you, most of the time? We think this question that has been at the heart of our research has potential for drawing teachers forward, together, in new ways toward imagining teaching in ways that encourage noticing, nurturing, and sustaining the path toward flourishing. We think this is a valuable and worthy pursuit and hope this book has enlivened your desire to pursue your own path toward flourishing.

We continue to be amazed at the extraordinary people who join with others in the high calling to be teachers. Their challenges are great, the cause is eternally worthwhile, and their commitment is phenomenal. We are in awe of the resolute good-will and self-sacrificing efforts of our colleagues. We realize this work is daunting. As we observe the education sector, we acknowledge that resources are diminishing; while demands are increasing. We are convinced that teacher wellbeing MUST be a priority for each teacher, regardless of where they are in their career cycle. We are convinced that teachers MUST continue to look up to and out for each other, especially with respect to supporting individual and collective wellbeing. We believe that teacher wellbeing is linked to student wellbeing. And we are convinced that there is a positive relationship between teacher wellbeing and flourishing schools. We are grateful for each reader who has considered the text of this book. Thank you for taking the time to read, try out new activities, reconnect with your own practices, and hopefully for sharing with others what you have been learning about what it means to flourish in your work. We wish you well as you continue on your important journey.

Chapter Eight

Epilogue for School Leaders

We want to begin this chapter with a loud and sincere *shout out* to those formal and informal school leaders who have offered themselves to further the sacred purposes of education. Co-creating the conditions and space for caring, trust, and hope in learning communities is a huge, multi-faceted responsibility. Leading entails cost and sacrifice; but it also has its rewards and affirmations. We believe that school leaders are a primary instrument, or levering factor, in the flourishing of schools and in the assurance of wellbeing for teachers, staff, students, and school families. Given the important influence of teachers on the wellbeing of their students, we know that we need to ensure that schools are places where teachers can be well, whole, happy, and engaged in their work—we suggest that creating these conditions is the primary work of leadership for flourishing schools. Administrators are critical for creating conditions for all (teachers, staff, students, and their families) to flourish, and so we have written this epilogue with the formal leaders within the school system in mind (principals, vice-principals, directors, and superintendents). Throughout the chapter we use the terms school leaders and administrators interchangeably to indicate those in positions of formal leadership throughout the school system. We hope that readers will note our unwavering claim that leadership for flourishing really is a collective mission. In this chapter, we bring to the forefront the critical role of the administrator as a levering factor, catalyzer, and champion for wellbeing in schools.

Noticing, Nurturing and Sustaining Flourishing: The Work of School Leaders

We hope that having read to this point, you'll know that our main passion is that every teacher will experience ongoing renewal in their understandings and practices; consistent, we hope, with the view that their own wellbeing, and the fostering of the wellbeing of those around them, are absolutely crucial game changers for their vocation. You'll have read that each teacher's ongoing wellbeing is fundamental to sustainable flourishing for themselves and others in their schools.

For the most part, school leaders are teachers, even if they don't always teach students. It is also okay to say that, for the most part, teachers are school leaders. In this epilogue, we want to feature school leaders who are leaders of leaders, servants of leaders, designated professional advocates for educational interests, and organizationally appointed stewards of educational resources and quality of learning in schools. The word "administrator" is broken down into the prefix "ad" (meaning "to" or "towards"), and "ministration" (meaning "to serve" or "to give aid"). To the extent that school leaders are "ad ministrators," they help make space for others to directly serve students, they energize, steer the collective services, and support individual and collective attention on agreed upon purposes. Additionally, administrators work to establish and sustain the various other priorities entailed in maintaining a vibrant learning community.

Recognizing that the work of formal school leaders is intense (and immense), we argue for placing and holding wellbeing at the heart of the work of administrators so that they may model, encourage, and facilitate wellbeing for all in their schools and systems. The virtuous cycle of wellbeing that our participants shared with us through their stories of flourishing—I flourish when my students do—can be spiralled out for administrators—I flourish when my teachers and their students do. We can think of no better way to spend a career than to ensure that all those around us are collectively engaged in the pursuit of flourishing with all those around them. So, in keeping with our original guiding question in this book we offer a question to focus your attention on wellbeing—what if the primary occupation for school leaders was to notice and nurture flourishing among their teachers?

The late, great, Thomas Sergiovanni (2005) said that school administrators have a special capacity to strengthen the heartbeat of their schools "to become stronger and more resilient" (p. 122). School administrators have the capacity to choose to foster communities of trust, hope, and interpersonal care, and to give priority to workplace wellbeing. He said,

> Conventional wisdom tells us that leadership is about finding solutions to problems that people face. In reality, leadership is more about helping people understand the problems they face, helping them manage these problems, and even helping them learn to live with them...few leaders have the competence, time, and information needed at any given time to get the job done. Wise leaders try to rely on others and build upon their leadership capacity. (p. 122)

We propose that the degree of vibrancy and thriving in a school setting will never be at a level higher than the aggregate and collective wellbeing of the teachers and staff who serve that community. We emphatically hold to the conviction that teachers hold the keys to school flourishing and, again, that the primary role of administrators and informal leaders is to co-create the workplace conditions for teachers to be at their best, in the fullest and most holistic sense of "best." Leaders can't "be" or "do" wellness for teachers; but everyday school leaders are difference-makers for the wellbeing of teachers. We are pained to say that it is also true that indifferent, incompetent, selfish, and toxic leaders can also be the profound sources and destructive forces contributing to teachers' dis-ease and un-wellness.

In this chapter, we encourage all administrators to work in ways such that teachers are well, get well, and stay well. In turn, teachers will facilitate the wellbeing of others. Overwhelmingly, we have been inspired and humbled by school leaders who are tireless in their efforts, characterized by compassion and passion for teacher wellbeing. We encourage them to not grow weary in their well-doing. We encourage them to attend to the messages we have stated throughout this book, and to take care of themselves so they can continue to maximize their noticing and nurturing of teacher wellbeing.

Flourishing Leadership: Creating Conditions for Positive Deviance

As we heard over and over again from the teachers in our research, how they experience their work—flourishing or not—is directly connected to the administrators in their school. Not surprisingly, when we talked with principals about when they feel a sense of being alive, engaged, whole, connected, and well in their work, the most common response was that they flourish when their teachers do. Creating conditions for teachers to thrive is satisfying and meaningful work; it requires thoughtful and ongoing attention to noticing and nurturing how others experience a sense of wellbeing in their work. As we have repeatedly mentioned, there is no formula or recipe for attaining wellbeing, since we will each experience flourishing in different ways and by different means. However, there are research-based approaches and strategies that leaders can use to ensure that wellbeing is at the center of their work, so that they are creating conditions where teachers may flourish most of the time.

From a positive organizational perspective, Cameron (2012) offered a model of leadership that emphasizes positive deviance (extraordinary work beyond common expectations); in other words, positive leadership. Positive leaders focus on strengths and affirm human potential (especially when faced with negative events), and they focus on the virtuousness within humans and their organizations (Cameron, 2012). The positive leadership model offers strategies that are useful for school leaders to notice and nurture wellbeing among their teachers—establishing positive communication, highlighting positive-meaning creating, growing positive relationships, and building a positive climate. For school leaders, we see how these four strategies are linked and intertwined, with each contributing to building and growing more of the others. We outline them here as opportunities and encouragements for administrators to create conditions for teachers to flourish by noticing the ways they can place, and hold, wellbeing for all at the heart of their work.

Positive Communication: Notice What You Can't See

Building a school culture where teachers can flourish requires that administrators pay careful attention to what is happening, but to also notice what we can't necessarily see. It is possible you might even recall the moment when you realized for the first time that something doesn't have to be visible or obvious to be real and to dramatically affect you. A lot of proactive and preventative stuff works like this: The stove doesn't look hot, but to interact with it like it isn't hot can cause major issues for us. A seemingly harmless joke or careless comment may stimulate visceral effects for someone who has hidden sensitivities. Sometimes words or actions will unexplainably trigger emotions in others, with no obvious explanation or apparent connection. Welcome to the complex world of humans! Developing school cultures where due care, due process, and due diligence are at the forefront, with a foresightedness that anticipates risks and requires action in order to reduce vulnerability and hurt, are part and parcel of the responsibilities of school leaders.

We enjoy the saying that "the problem with communication is that it is too often assumed to have taken place." Positive communication requires timely and appropriate feedback; look, for example, at this fictitious story of a principal who had told a teacher ten years earlier that she was impressed by her [the teacher's] work with students. When asked if, as principal, she had provided more recent comments or feedback, she responded, "no, if I change my mind, I'll let her know." Yikes! What is communicated by our silences?

An important aspect of teacher wellbeing is knowing that they are making a positive difference in the lives of students, their families, and for others in the school. Administrators can play a big role in building positive communication by acknowledging teachers' difference-making, and modeling for them how to encourage positive communication with their colleagues. One principal from our study shared that she was trying to build wellbeing and a positive climate with the teachers by starting every staff meeting with a round of "orchids"—positive messages about what had been working well for them or what they had noticed from others. She made time for the "onions" as well (the term she used for those events and moments that may induce tears); however, she always started with the orchids to boost the mood and ensure that teachers knew that their good works were noticed. This practice reflects Cameron's (2008) assertion that leaders should be aware of, and aim to bolster against, the negativity bias that is inherent in all humans and human systems. This bias means that we tend to be hardwired to notice and pay attention to negative messages and events more strongly than the positive ones. To counter this bias, school leaders aiming to build and maintain positive communication in their schools emphasize positive events and messages, whether as individual feedback or systemic systems such as staff meeting conversations. Positive leaders do not deny negative events, and do not turn away from the need for feedback that may not be positive, but they are mindful of the potential of positive emotions to grow more of what is wanted, and so use this to their advantage to grow positive communication throughout the school.

While we can do our best to build and sustain positive communication, we have all experienced the phenomenon of unintended consequences. Sometimes the best intended actions or words are completely turned on their heads, resulting in twisted, unrecognized or unanticipated experiences. This can be puzzling, surprising, embarrassing, and can be difficult to recover from. Our personal and professional experiences grow our attentions, and, where possible, we hope to learn from these experiences in ways that increasingly mitigate or minimize these unpleasant or unanticipated occurrences.

Positive Meaning: Being Wide-Awake to Our Impact

It is interesting that sometimes we underestimate our influence, and sometimes we overestimate our influence. Most of the time we have no idea of the deep and enduring effects from our engagement with others. In our years working with school leaders, we've realized that some have been unaware of their profound influence and the impact that they have had on those they have served. As indicated, impacts and influences can be positive or negative; they can be helpful or harmful. We have heard many stories of administrators who were oblivious to the difference that omissions (often subtle and/or nuanced), tiny acts, or particular words have made on their teacher colleagues.

One of the ways that school leaders can create conditions for teachers to flourish is to help them to see the impact of their actions, the meaning in their work, the bigger purpose to which they are contributing. Again, we urge administrators to contribute to building Leaderful Mindsets within the school by modeling for teachers to be leaders for and with others; leading for positive meaning is such an opportunity. In our conversations with principals, they experienced flourishing when they worked with their teachers to build learning cultures of deep purpose, where they knew they were all working together toward important goals, and felt they were all making a difference in their students' lives. We have found that creating conditions for teachers to experience meaning and purpose in their work often happens through collaborative teaching arrangements; the work of the administrator is often to encourage and champion teachers' explorations of new ways of teaching, and create time, space, and other organizational structures that ensure these collaborative opportunities.

Administrators who notice and nurture teachers' wellbeing through attending to positive meaning often have a strong sense of meaning in their own work and life. They model what it can look like to work from a place of passion and purpose, sharing with others their values and sense of meaning, and modeling for them the satisfaction and joy that comes from working through, and for, deep meaning.

Positive Relationships: Empathetic School Leaders

Some of the most effective school leaders we know are the ones who run interference and advocate for their teachers. By running interference, we mean that they help teachers avoid goal displacement or get side-tracked and side-swiped by the avalanches of demands that can beset teachers. By advocating for teachers, we mean speaking out for teachers in timely and supportive ways, without necessarily speaking for them or operating in paternalistic or patronizing modes. Effective and empathetic school leaders are able to **step-in, step-back, step-away, and step-up,** with remarkable timing and sensitivity. They signal to others that their leaderful social radars are working (that they have emotional and social intelligence). These strategies contribute to building relationships of trust, where teachers know and see that their administrator is working to ensure they can carry out their work in the best way possible.

When teachers are being assailed by certain people, pressures, or petty tasks, the school leader **steps-in** and helps out. When teachers are under stress and need air, need supervision-free space, need room to make mistakes without an audience, need "processing time," or need room to innovate, create—or even re-create—these leaders **step-back**. They know how and when to **step-away** and give wide-berth to teachers who need the more real estate. They also act a bit like a traffic cop, as they direct others away from teachers who need the room to manoeuver, recuperate, or mature their life worlds or circumstances. It is inspiring to hear about and observe school leaders who have **stepped-up** for teachers; they do this with well-timed words of encouragement, a word to the wise, or a word of thanks or recognition. Words, simple words, can be transformative: "leave it to me, I'll get that done for you," "you are terrific," "that was so appreciated," "what do you need from me to move this forward," "you are so valuable to our team," "I love it when...," "take a breath; take a 'breather," and "what can I do to support you as you are going through this personal stuff?" Empathetic school leaders make it their mission to step-in, step-back, step-away, and step up.

Fundamental to empathetic and efficacious leadership and effective teamship, according to Koffman and Senge (1993), is the creation of "spaces for generative conversations and concerted action, where people can talk from their hearts and connect with one another in the spirit of dialogue...[to create] a field of alignment that produces tremendous power to invent new realities...and to bring about these new realities in action" (p. 16). For the wellbeing of both leaders and teachers to be sustained, colleagues must be grounded in at least three foundations: a school culture that is rooted in generative human values and committed to the value of everyone's wellbeing; a set of practices for life-giving conversation and coordinated regenerative action; and a capacity to see work, play, wellness and learning intertwined (Koffman & Senge, 1993, p. 11).

We certainly don't want to set school leaders up as the singular factor or sole guardians of teacher wellbeing, because that would be an overstated distortion and unfair attribution. However, empathetic, empowering, and practically supportive school leaders build and maintain strong, positive relations with their teachers, and this matters significantly. Teachers from our research shared with us their appreciation and valuing of working with administrators who are making overt efforts to notice and nurture wellbeing in the lives of their teachers. They feel a sense of being cared for, of belonging to a community (that, at its best, feels like a family), and they feel known and valued. These positive relationships reap exponential rewards in the life of the school as teachers pay this forward to their students, and to each other. When school leaders communicate that teacher wellbeing is vital, teachers feel encouraged and empowered to notice and nurture their own and others' wellbeing—a virtuous cycle of vitality.

Positive Climate: Knowing, Caring for, and Nurturing Teachers

Building a positive climate means fostering compassion, gratitude, and forgiveness (Cameron, 2012), and growing workplace conditions where teachers feel a strong sense of caring and trust. As we have shared throughout this book, teachers flourish when they work in a climate of deep care and support, and where they feel safe to innovate and try out new practices in their teaching. In these positive climates, they enjoy fun times with their colleagues, and they also experience a level of trust that they work in an environment where they can share with their administrators, and with each other, when their teaching (or another aspect of their life) is not going as well as they would hope. There is a level of acceptance and grace for mistakes and making amends. Teachers feel known, cared for, and challenged to grow and thrive in their teaching.

Leading to build a positive climate is about co-creating a reciprocal relationship of equals with different roles, working to help each other succeed with the life-long and life-wide achievement of mutual purposes, sharing superordinate values, and other benefiting promises. It is about the creation of synergistic, symbiotic, serendipitous, and people-sensitive conditions for the wellbeing of everyone in the school community. The leader who pays attention, who can see the unspoken, and who is able to know each teacher's skills, talents, temperaments, passions, and giftedness, the leader who asks second questions (i.e., after "how are you doing"), who cares for each teacher's overall wellbeing—this is the leader living out positive leadership in ways that facilitate the co-creation of an environment of flourishing for teachers.

Nurturing Teacher Wellbeing

We can't think of a group of people better placed, educated, and experienced as school leaders for nurturing teacher wellbeing. Educators know that nurturance is important, and how to do it; this is what education and learning is all about. As many readers will know, when you want grass or plants to grow, you need to appreciate what are the most suitable, multi-nutrient fertilizers for particular plants, soil, and conditions. "NPK fertilizers" provide nitrogen, phosphorus and potassium in certain prescribed proportions; when you purchase your fertilizer you'll see three numbers describing the amount or percentage of each chemical (i.e., 16-4-8). Our point is that one size does not fit all (even if this might be more administratively convenient if it did!). Each teacher will need a unique formulation for their wellbeing and thriving to be sustained.

Here is an interesting, unscientific, and speculative formula that we'd suggest for administrators. We offer a 90-7-3 approach to the practices of leading. While these numbers are made-up, the proportions are our way of communicating a sense of the magnitude of each of these important ingredients. Still, every teacher will require a different formulation. You might want to see these numbers as three forms of Vitamin E: Encouragement (Vitamin E1), exhortation (Vitamin E2), and enlightenment (Vitamin E3). Our point is that encouragement is the greatest tool in the hands and hearts of school leaders to support the wellbeing of teachers; exhortation and enlightenment are valuable but lesser tools. Here is a modest set of illustrative thoughts for school leaders' to consider, in a fashion complementary to, and affirming of, their own approaches to teacher support.

Encouragement (ninety percent)

We suggest that 90% of support for teacher wellbeing comes from words and deeds of encouragement from their administrators. As you will have heard, our words can bring life and they can destroy. "En" means "in" or "within," and "courage" means to speak one's mind by telling all one's heart. Simply speaking, to encourage is to add courage into another's life. Sometimes encouragement comes by listening and asking questions, sometimes by specific words spoken, messages conveyed or actions displayed.

We have already foreshadowed much of what we want to say to administrators about encouragement as a way of supporting the longings of teachers and their wellbeing. Words are powerful means of encouragement. We suggest that there are at the very least two words for the frequent and authentic use of school leaders: "**YES**," and "**WOW**."

We've asked school leaders: Are you seen by others to be a "yes" person or a "cold bucket of water" person? "Yes people" will find ways to make things happen. They are solution-finders, rather than problem-finders. Leaders who are "yes-leaning" find ways to give teachers a break, to pay for and pave their ways. They know that whole people (complex, multi-dimensional, complicated people) walk into the school. These teachers carry a lot with them as they move in and out of school days, and back and forth between homes and workplaces. An affirming "yes" to a teachers' self-care efforts is an investment in today and tomorrow.

Then there are those who feel they must carry around water buckets to drench the fires of enthusiasm with the weight of bureaucratic hoops or their self-appointed paternalistic ways (adult to child transactions). In the extreme, "water bucket people" send negative vibes, and teachers eventually just know that something to criticize or belittle will be found with their each and every, big and small, initiative. By the way, every good idea will have something wrong with it. These bucket folks just seem to relish their ability to find holes in ideas in creative ways, and effectively rain on parades before they can even get going.

On the other hand, there are those who are energizers. Our current work is focused on positive school leaders who fit this bill. These are the "yes people" in teachers' lives and workplaces. With a wink, they agree to address the shortcomings, even ignore the imperfections, but see the potential; they affirm teachers, their passions and their pursuits for making things better, including ways to keep themselves well. In a way, there is an almost playful approach to—and with—the negatives that are evident in every person and in every situation. There is much mileage to be gained from a well-placed "yes." We grant that saying "yes" is often more work; it entails making exceptions, requires balancing and managing perceptions, requires staying on top of politics, and making a case to those who hold the keys to the implementation of the proposal in question. Saying "yes" can mean spending the leader's social capital on behalf of another, and risking being misunderstood. We aren't advocating laissez-faire leading or doormat acquiescence; we are asking, if we've listened deeply to the teacher's request (explicit or implicit), need, or proposal, can we imagine a way to say "yes?"

Next, regarding the second critical word as a means of encouragement, we suggest that administrators revisit their lexicon of **"Wow"** words and find measured but non-reluctant ways to sprinkle these expressions among teachers. What might it take for us to recover any lost sense of child-like wonder we have in terms of witnessing the incredible people in our lives and workplaces. We suggest that there is an over supply of deficit-noticers in some of our schools today. Through our research to understand what it means to flourish in schools, we have been awe-filled so often as we've walked into classrooms, into assemblies, down hallways, into professional development sessions, or engaged in small groups or personal conversations with teachers. The closer we've listened to their stories, the more in awe we have become. Our awe is often articulated as "WOW." As we read through the transcripts of our conversations with teachers, we were delighted to see the numbers of audible "wows" recorded! We've noticed brilliance, resilience, passion, giftedness, compassion, competence, vision, and skills that are simply amazing. "Wow" is a way of appreciating and recognizing.

Wow can describe good things and hard things (awful good and awful bad), but the sense is that it resonates as an expression of profound realization. Awe can be spoken of as a feeling of reverential respect, or a concoction of pain, grief, dread, terror, and admiration, all wrapped together. Awe can displace our feigned rationality and our impoverished adult (or so we think) sophistication. The non-awe stuff in life is said to be inspired by narcissism, materialism, cynicism, social mimicry, disconnection, despair, deficit thinking, and hallowed out, false narratives. "Wow" just recognizes awe, and is like deep gratitude and compassion—important ingredients for growing a positive climate.

Our expressions of "wow" are unlike so many self-focused emotions because awe goes beyond us to connect with the magic, the mystery, the strength, the perseverance, and the something special in life. Researchers have demonstrated that when awe is experienced and "wow" is announced, this complex emotion improves health, increases pro-social behaviour (kindness, self-sacrifice, cooperation, volunteerism, resource-sharing), enhances curiosity, improves critical and creative thinking, expands our perception of time (brings us into the moment), influences decisions, and makes life more satisfying. Wow!

Administrators are great clarions of encouragement, and they will have many, many ways of custom-making their encouragements for particular teachers and circumstances. Indeed, encouragement is a powerful tool for supporting teacher wellbeing.

Exhortation (seven percent)

Exhortation is another powerful tool for administrators in their efforts to foster teacher wellbeing. While this is not a common concept in our vocabularies, we think administrators do this very well. If you think of horticulture, you think of creating environments and approaches for effectively growing things (that is the "hort" part of exhortation). The "ex" prefix is about "drawing out of." An exhortation is communicating or influencing in an emphatic way that urges or persuades someone to do something. We may be taking license with meaning but we prefer to view exhortation, in the context of this book, as administrators doing whatever makes sense to compel teachers to take care of themselves and others; to respectfully admonish or convince teachers to pay attention to what is working for them and figure out what is not working, especially in terms of their personal and professional wellbeing and growth.

There is so much we might say here, but we will limit this to two points: mentoring by questions and challenging by truth-telling.

Elsewhere (Sanga & Walker, 2011) we've expanded on the so-called maieutic method of **mentorship**. This approach was popularized by Mortimer Alder (1982), in *The Paideia proposal: An educational manifesto.* He described the work of school leader-mentors as metaphorical mid-wives who draw out from each teacher what the teacher already knows but needs help to deliver. How is this done? Able administrators and teacher colleagues ask great questions. This approach avoids telling, presumption, and quick fixes, and instead sees the dignity, brilliance, and latent power of a teacher's soul, as capable of discovering, reflecting on, and uncovering self-assessment, fitting remedies and best courses of action. Of course there are many types of questions for the array of circumstances of mentorship. This is evocative work. This is co-journeying and human accompaniment. If the destination is noticing, nurturing, and sustaining wellbeing, the leader comes alongside, by earned invitation, to join in the interdependent quest.

From time to time, **truth-telling** and candor by administrators are needed. As teachers move along the spectrum or continuum of wellbeing, from feeling a sense of flourishing to feeling a sense of languishing, there is a higher tendency to give into unhealthy patterns of thought and false narratives. Self-deprecation, re-runs of worst moments, or humiliating distortions of one's own dignity and worth can play out. Teachers (and administrators too, of course) can become their own worst enemies and give foothold to false, biased, or distorted internal stories or scripts. Certain circumstances or experiences can result in teachers becoming gripped with fear and the desire to run away, hide and isolate themselves.

Negative self-talk and self-punishing behaviour is more prevalent that one might think. Unwittingly, subtle, and even unconscious, harmful or hindering inner narratives can be written onto the hearts of both administrators and teachers. Mean-spirited comments can be made and much damage can be done. Teachers can give up on themselves, refuse to forgive their own mistakes, forget their victories, underestimate their positive influence, and become discouraged, even despairing. The positive leadership strategy of fostering forgiveness, compassion, and gratitude can be an antidote to these states; the soothing, courage-bearing, and truth-telling school leader can intervene, mediate, broker, bargain, and work with teachers to displace the fears that are hindering, and even paralyzing, them. Caring for teachers in ways that lets them see (and to re-see, over and over again) their own goodness, strengths, contributions, and value, helping them to craft stories of passion and purpose, of fun and enjoyment, even when they are struggling and challenged to see the meaning and worth of themselves and their work—these are essential and vital ways leaders can support their teachers toward noticing and nurturing wellbeing.

Enlightenment (three percent)

From time to time, administrators will bring wisdom, perspective, and enlightenment into the purview of teachers. They will share a discovery, provide feedback, playback a situation, or express what they see "from the balcony." The gift of insights, discernments, objectivity, distance, untangled sight lines, and non-enmeshed positioning can be altogether helpful to teacher wellbeing. We are fond of the saying that "teachers don't care how much you know until they know how much you care." Simply trying to fix teachers with what we think we know is a fated approach to support. This said, administrators can often comfort those with similar comfort that they, themselves, have experienced. We are mindful that "com" is "to have in common" and "fort" means strength; so to comfort another is to be strong together with them.

We think that administrators have a huge role to play in speaking truth to power. School systems can become impersonal. Administrators can remind those who are making "people decisions" from afar what it is like on the front lines. They can advocate through efforts to enlighten policy makers and policy keepers. People tend to be down on what they are not up on—so school leaders can and should inform, influence, and persuade funders, employee assistance providers, human resources officers, and union representatives. Administrators can make sure no teacher falls between the cracks, and, if permission is granted, they can speak for particular wellbeing needs of teachers. Some teaching setups are intolerable, and teachers are sometimes not well-positioned to say so. Administrators can be equity champions, wellbeing promoters, and purveyors of hope and the best interests for each and every person in the learning community. Teachers need fair and just treatment, and there are times for administrators to intervene to make sure this happens. As we've said, there may be times when school leaders need to take some risks, shake some trees, rock some boats, or stir some pots (choose whatever metaphor you prefer). Being a school leader isn't about being popular—it's more about serving those you work with and making sure they know they are significant and safe, that they know their wellbeing is important to everyone, and that they are reminded that they belong and that the work they do is unspeakably important. We are convinced that administrators can make extraordinary contributions to the wellbeing of teachers.

Shifting Ground: Noticing and nurturing wellbeing with circles of attention

If you are an informal or formal school leader (we think this exercise is useful for any adult in a school), try this shifting ground activity. We've chosen this one tool from our process kit because of its focus on a leader's efforts to notice and nurture teacher wellbeing.

Book a half-hour appointment with yourself (actually put the appointment in your calendar). When the appointed time comes, put your smart phone on airplane mode, find a comfortable chair, and sit with a note pad and pen in hand. Take a few minutes to breath; take time to "bracket" your busyness and displace it with some ease. When your "insides" are slowed down, draw a large circle in the middle of the page with your first name in the middle of the circle. Ask yourself how you are doing from a wellbeing perspective, in general, and over the last day or two. Are you suffering (0-3), struggling (4-6), or thriving (7-10)? Put down a number between 1 and 10 beside your name. Reflect on this for a few minutes. Why this number? Any parts of your life-space that might be bringing the number up or down? Sit with this, and then ask yourself what number you think the people who care for you, and know you best, would assign to you if asked the same question. Jot that second number down beside your name, perhaps with a backslash after the first number. Are there any notable differences? Do others see you the same way you see yourself? Take a moment or two to contemplate and unpack what these numbers might represent.

In the same circle put the initials of five or six teachers with whom you've had specific connections in the last few days. One at a time, and without hurry, what is your best guess of how each might see their own general wellbeing (think of your last interactions with them). Put down a number beside their name. What do you see that explains how you see this person's state of wellbeing? Of course this isn't about judgment; it's about empathy and radar-like sensitivity. Now, before you move onto the next person, send some good thoughts or prayers out for this colleague and consider how you might practically encourage them over the next week.

After you have given the colleagues inside the circle your attention, bring to mind 5 or 6 teachers who you would consider to be the ones you are currently least connected to. Put their initials on the outside of the circle. Ask yourself why these teachers are on the outside (choice, circumstances, interpersonal distance, a critical event-history, mutual or unilateral preference, or whatever). Ask yourself who among the members of your learning community are more connected to these teachers. Do any of these teachers appear friendless or isolated? After thinking about why they are on the outside, and who among those on your inside might have connections with them, ask yourself if there is anything you might do to support them? Consider what questions you might ask to find out what that person might need for their wellbeing that might be supported by closer colleagues, or yourself? If you aren't sure about any of this, decide to be mindful of them and their best interests in the days to come. By the way, we want to remind you

> that just as it is natural for a classroom teacher to give more attention to certain students, it can be natural for some colleagues to garner more attention - and of course, conversely, for some to get less; school leaders need to consider ways that could bring the colleague going unnoticed into at least one or two colleague's range of awareness and support.

≈

This socio-gram (or socio-graph) is a great tool for awareness and strategy. We know some school leaders who use and adapt this simple tool to reflect on teachers' strengths and passions. For example, for half of the staff, put their names in the circle and write one or two words beside each to describe that person's strength, talent, passion, or giftedness. Notice how much you know about their strengths and passions. What about the other half of staff members? Others have used the tool by putting teachers' names down and drawing lines (thick and thin) between each name to indicate known collaborations, common interests, influences, or interactions (even indicating breaks or difficulties in relations).

Flourishing Leadership for Teacher Wellbeing

Each of us is energized and drained by different things. Leaders need to openly have conversations with teachers to find out what works and what doesn't. Flourishing leadership is the pursuit of finding out what the teacher needs—to be, to do, to grow, and take chances—then working with them to create the conditions for these optimal needs to be provided. Everyone wins under this kind of arrangement.

In this chapter, we have provided insights and strategies for you to think about positive leadership for noticing and nurturing teacher wellbeing. Growing flourishing can happen, teacher-by-teacher, as administrators use lots of encouragement, a little exhortation, and a bit of enlightenment, to create positive climates where teacher wellbeing is prioritized. Positive school leaders who aim to grow conditions for flourishing will attend to building positive climates where compassion, forgiveness, and gratitude are wonderfully rampant. They will build positive communication capacities for and with teachers, and they will work with teachers to help them see the positive meaning in their work, especially when they are unable to see it themselves. Leadership for flourishing is the important work of school leaders. As we have suggested throughout this book, we think this call to action for wellbeing needs to be at the heart of the work of teaching, learning, and leading in schools—it is the work of our time. Our hope is that you hear this call to action, and the encouragement in these pages, to continue to support the wellbeing of teachers. We hope your attentions, choices, actions, and priorities, resonate with the logic that school administrators and informal school leaders can, and do, make major positive contributions to the work-lives and overall wellbeing of teachers by focusing on doing all that they can to support teacher health and thriving. The logic continues by asserting that healthy and thriving teachers overflow in their capacity to foster the desirable features in their students (happiness, health, and learning vitality). By combining noticing, nurturing, and sustaining attention, with action on teacher wellbeing, school communities flourish, learning is enhanced, and schools improve in wonderful ways.

Afterword

Sabre and Keith have invited us to imagine workplaces in which we thrive, and that support the flourishing of the other adults and young people who inhabit these school spaces as well. They note that too many educators have become weary in their "well-doing," and thus extend an invitation for us to explore educator "wellbeing." They frame this invitation by asking us to ponder "what if": what if we were to imagine that our *primary roles* as educators is to learn how to thrive in our roles, and, in so doing, to continually explore and facilitate all means by which each person in our learning community flourishes along with us? Their thesis in this exploration is that "happy, healthy, and whole [educators] provide strong support for happy, healthy, and whole children and youth" (p. 8).

The wellbeing Sabre and Keith hope to bring about in schools is about noticing, nurturing, and sustaining human flourishing by attending to positive emotions, strong relationships, a felt sense of meaning and purpose, deep engagement, and the satisfaction that comes with achievement. They encourage us to establish guideposts for maintaining a focus on wellbeing in our workplaces through noticing, nurturing, and sustaining those dynamics that contribute to flourishing. By *noticing* where we feel a sense of flourishing at work, and capturing experiences and moments where we feel well, engaged, alive, and on purpose, we can then determine what we might want to do to *nurture* and grow this sense of flourishing through structuring our work in ways that connect us more frequently with other people, and that provide access to resources that promote our wellbeing. We might engage in this work either alone or with colleagues in order to establish structures, habits, relationships, ceremonies, and celebrations for *sustaining* this sense of flourishing for ourselves and others in the school.

Throughout the book, Sabre and Keith have offered powerful images and enticing visions of supportive and collaborative workplaces filled with laughter, fun, and joy. They present a helpful model to guide our thinking about flourishing in schools centered on fostering compassion, trust, and hope, as expressed through "leaderful" mindsets (calling forth the leader in all of us), adaptive community, and wellbeing. Compassion induces a desire to act in a generous way towards all human beings in an effort to alleviate physical or emotional suffering (p. 73). Trust has to do with feeling a sense of ease and confidence in a situation of interdependence in bringing about outcomes that are important to us, such as supporting the development of the young people in our care (Tschannen-Moran, 2014). Hope is about conjuring a desired future and knowing that we can play a role in creating a new reality that better aligns with who we hope to be, both individually and collectively (p. 77). The shift that Sabre and Keith describe, and hope to bring about for those who read this book, is toward noticing and fostering the positive human capabilities in schools, such as love, courage, wisdom, kindness, and compassion.

Keith and Sabre don't just describe their "flourishing pedagogy"; they invite us, as readers, to engage in experiential learning through their Heart Prints and Shifting Ground exercises. Heart Prints are moments for noticing our own emotional reactions to the images and information we are receiving, and to reflect on how to integrate those visions with our own lived experiences. Their Shifting Ground exercises are "creative pit stops" that remind us that change can be disorienting, even when it is in the direction of greater flourishing. Even if at first we simply read through these exercises without actually engaging, we can go back to them as resources whenever the longing for greater flourishing wells up in us.

Appreciative inquiry is a process that shines a light on a school's strengths, core values, purposes, and aspirations. It is an especially valuable tool to guide us in our collective imaginings of schools that support human flourishing. This is a process that has been widely used around the globe in other sectors of the economy; it enjoys a solid and growing research base, and yet is not well known in education. The underlying premise, that we can enact organizational change not through an investigation of our deficits but instead through an exploration of our successes and strengths, goes against our taken-for-granted notions of organizational change. And yet, it again and again has proven to be an effective means to shift schools, even those experiencing significant challenges, in a positive direction. School leaders can *initiate* the process by settling on a topic (or a set of topics) for inquiry, and making a conscious choice to adopt a strengths-based orientation. They then invite a broad base of stakeholders to *inquire* into their successes, values, and aspirations in the area of inquiry. Next, participants *imagine* their school as it would be if it built on these strengths to more closely meet their aspirations. They then *innovate* their way into new policies and practices, only to frame a new question for inquiry and start the process all over again. The *Power of Appreciative Inquiry,* by Diana Whitney and Amanda Trosten-Bloom (2010), is a helpful guide for those interested in exploring this process in greater depth.

Teacher Wellbeing: Noticing, Nurturing, Sustaining, and Flourishing in Schools contributes to a small but growing literature on positive organizational scholarship in schools. It offers hope for those who are longing for schools to foster life-giving and vibrant spaces in which students and educators alike will flourish. By giving us language for the longings that many feel but few are able to adequately express, Keith and Sabre have brought this new reality a significant step closer to being realized.

Megan Tschannen-Moran
October 2017

Dr. Megan Tschannen-Moran is teacher, founding and long-standing principal (low socio-economic area of Chicago), professor, and major contributor to the scholarship of teaching, learning, leadership, and coaching. Megan's books, ***Trust Matters*** *and* ***Evocative Coaching*** *(co-authored with her husband Bob), are outstanding resources for educators. Professor Tschannen-Moran is well-known around the world for her research and writing on teachers' self-efficacy and the connections between teacher behaviour and student outcomes. Through her own positive and appreciative practice, she is a wonderful colleague and incredible encouragement to many.*

References

Achor, S. (2011). *The happiness advantage: The seven principles of positive psychology that fuel success and performance at work.* New York, NY: Crown Business.

Adler, M. (1982). *The Paideia proposal: An educational manifesto.* New York, NY: Macmillan.

Allender, J., & Allender, D. S. (2008). *The humanistic teacher: First the child, then curriculum.* Boulder, CO: Paradigm Publishers.

Apple, M., & Beane, J. (2007). *Democratic schools: Lessons in powerful education* (2nd Ed.). New York, NY: Routledge.

Baldwin, C. (2005). *Storycatcher: Making sense of our lives through the power and practice of story.* Novato, CA: New World Library.

Bermejo-Toro, L. Prieto-Ursúa, M., & Hernández, V. (2016) Towards a model of teacher wellbeing: Personal and job resources involved in teacher burnout and engagement. *Educational Psychology, 36*(3), p. 481-501, DOI: 10.1080/01443410.2015.1005006

Binfet, J.T. (2015). Not-so random acts of kindness: A guide to intentional kindness in the classroom. *International Journal of Emotional Education*, 7(2), 49-62.

Binfet, J.T., Gaderman, A.M., & Schonert-Reichl, K.A. (2016). Measuring kindness at school: Psychometric properties of a school kindness scale for children and adolescents. *Psychology in Schools*, 53(2), 111-126.

Block, P. (2009). *Community: The structure of belonging.* San Francisco, CA: Berrett-Kohler.

Brown, W., & Cherkowski, S. (2011). Owning our learning: Scaffolding professional inquiry for teachers. *LEARNing Landscapes,* 4(2), 61-78.

Cameron, K. (2008). *Positive leadership: Strategies for extraordinary performance.* San Francisco, CA: Berrett-Koehler Publishers.

Cameron, K. S., & Caza, A. (2004). Introduction: Contributions to the discipline of positive organizational scholarship. *The American Behavioral Scientist, 47(6), 731-739.*

Capra, F. (2004). *The hidden connections: Integrating the biological, cognitive, and social dimensions of life into a science of sustainability*. New York, NY: Doubleday.

Carmona, C., Buunk, A., Peiro, J., Rodrigues, I., & Bravo, M. (2006). Do social comparison and coping styles play a role in the development of burnout? Cross-sectional and longitudinal findings. *Journal of Occupational and Organizational Psychology, 79*, 85-99.

Cherkowski, S. (2016). The role of the school principal in cultivating professional learning climates. *Journal of School Leadership*, 26(3), 523-543.

Cherkowski, S. (2012). Teacher commitment in sustainable learning communities: A new "ancient" story of educational leadership. *Canadian Journal of Education,* 35(1), 56-68.

Cherkowski, S., Kutsyuruba, B., & Walker, K. (2015). Principals' moral agency and ethical decision-making: Towards transformative ethics. *International Journal of Educational Policy and Leadership*, 10(3), 1-17.

Cherkowski, S., & Ragoonaden, K. (2016). Leadership for diversity: Intercultural communication competence as professional development. *Teacher Learning and Professional Development*, 1(1), 33-43.

Cherkowski, S., & Schnellert, L. (2017a). Exploring teacher leadership in a rural, secondary school: Reciprocal learning teams as a catalyst for emergent leadership. *International Journal of Teacher Leadership*, 8(1), 6-25.

Cherkowski, S., & Schnellert, L. (2017b). Professional learning communities as emergent, responsive learning teams. *Teacher Development*, 22(2), 229-248.

Cherkowski, S., & Walker, K. (2016). Flourishing leadership: Engaging purpose, passion, and play in the work of leading schools. *Journal of Educational Administration,* 54 (4), 378-392.

Cherkowski, S., & Walker, K. (2014). Flourishing communities: Re-storying educational leadership using a positive research lens. *International Journal of Leadership in Education: Theory and Practice, 17*(2), 200-217.

Cherkowski, S., & Walker, K. (2013a). Schools as sites of human flourishing: Musing on an inquiry into efforts to foster sustainable learning communities. *Journal of Educational Administration and Foundations, 23*(2), 139-154.

Cherkowski, S., & Walker, K. (2013b). Living the flourishing question: Positivity as an orientation for the preparation of teacher candidates. *Northwest Journal of Teacher Education, 11*(2), 80-103.

Cherkowski, S., Hanson, K. & Walker, K. (in press). Flourishing in adaptive community: Balancing structures and flexibilities. *Journal of Professional Capital and Community.*

Cherkowski, S., Hanson, K., & Walker, K. (2018). *Mindful Alignment: Foundations of educator flourishing.* Lanham, MD: Lexington.

Clandinin, D. J., & Connelly, F. M. (1996). Teachers' professional knowledge landscapes: Teacher stories-stories of teachers, school stories-stories of schools. *Educational Researcher*, 25, 24–30.

Cochran-Smith, M., & Lytle, S. L. (Eds.). (2009). *Inquiry as stance: Practitioner research for the next generation.* New York, NY: Teachers College Press.

Cohen, J. (Ed.) (2001). *Caring classrooms/intelligent schools: The social emotional education of young children.* New York, NY: Teacher's College Press.

Cooperrider, D. n.d. http://appreciativeinquiry.case.edu/

Cooperrider, D. & Godwin, L. (2011). Positive organization development: Innovation-inspired change in an economy and ecology of strengths. *Oxford Handbook of Positive Organizational Scholarship*, pp. 737-750. Oxford, UK: Oxford University Press.

Cooperrider, D., & Srivastva, S. (2013). *Organizational generativity: The appreciative inquiry summit and a scholarship of transformation.* In R. Woodman & W. Pasmore (Eds.), pp. 3-7. London, UK: Emerald.

Cooperrider, D. L., & Srivastva, S. (1987). Appreciative Inquiry in Organizational Life. In W. Pasmore & R. Woodman (Eds.), *Research in Organization Change and Development*, pp. 129-169. Greenwich, CT: JAI Press.

Csikszentmihalyi, M. (1997). *Finding flow: The psychology of engagement with everyday life.* New York, NY: Basic Books.

Day, C., Sammons, P., Stobart, G., & Kingston, A. Qing Gu. (2007). *Teachers matter: Connecting lives, work and effectiveness.* Berkshire, UK: Open University Press.

Deci, E. L., & Ryan, R. M. (2012). Motivation, personality, and development within embedded social contexts: An overview of self-determination theory. In R. Ryan (Ed.). *The Oxford Handbook of Human Motivation* (pp. 85rd Han Oxford: Oxford University Press

DePree, M. (1989). *Leadership is an art.* New York: Doubleday.

Diener, E. (2000). Subjective wellbeing: The science of happiness and a proposal for a national index. *American Psychologist,* 55(1), 34-43.

Diener, E., & Seligman, M. (2004). Beyond money. *Psychological Science in the Public Interest,* 5(1), 1-31.

Diener, Ed. (1984). Subjective wellbeing. In Ed Diener (Ed.), *The Science of wellbeing: The collected works of Ed Diener:* Social Indicators Research Series, Volume 37 (pp. 11-58). London, UK: Springer.

Drago-Severson, E. (2009). Leading adult learning: Supporting adult development in our schools. Thousand Oaks, CA: Corwin.

Dutton, J.E. (2003). *Energize your workplace: How to create and sustain high quality connections in your workplace.* San Francisco, CA: Jossey-Bass.

Dutton, J. E., & Heaphy, E. D. (2003). The power of high-quality connections. *Positive organizational scholarship: Foundations of a new discipline, 3,* 263-278.

Dutton, J. E., Worline, M. C., Frost, P. J., & Lilius, J. (2006). Explaining compassion organizing. *Administrative Science Quarterly, 51*(1), 59-96.

Dweck, C. (2006). *Mindset. The new psychology of success: How we can learn to fulfill our potential.* New York, NY: Random House.

Elias, M. J., & Arnold, H. (Eds.). (2006). *The educator's guide to emotional intelligence and academic achievement.* Thousand Oaks, CA: Corwin Press.

Fredrickson, B. (2008). Promoting positive affect. In M. Eid & R. Larsen (Eds.), *The Science of Subjective Wellbeing* (pp. 449–468). New York, NY: Guildford Press.

Fredrickson, B. L., & Losada, M. F. (2005). Positive affect and the complex dynamics of human flourishing. *American Psychologist,* 60, 678–686.

Fernet, C., Guay, F., Senecal, C., & Austin, S. (2012). Predicting intraindividual changes in teacher burnout: The role of perceived school environment and motivational factors. *Teaching and Teacher Education, 28,* 514-525.

Feuerhahn, N., Stamov-RoBnagel, C., Wolfram, M., Bellingrath, S., & Kudielka, B. (2013). Emotional exhaustion and cognitive performance in apparently health teachers: A longitudinal multi-source study. *Stress and Health, 29,* 297-306.

Froeschle, J., & Crews, C. (2010). Examining teachers' perspectives of creative relaxation. *Journal of Creativity in Mental Health, 5,* 290-304.

Frost, P., Dutton, J., Worline M., & Wilson, A. (2000). Narratives of compassion in organizations. In S. Fineman (Ed.), *Emotions in Organizations* (pp. 25-45). London: Sage Publications.

Furman, G.C. (2004). The ethic of community. *Journal of Educational Administration*, (42) 2, 215-235.

Gergen, K. (1999/2015). *An invitation to social construction*. 3rd Ed. Thousand Oaks, CA: Sage.

Giroux, H. (2015). *Schooling and the struggle for public life: Democracy's promise and education's challenge* (2nd ed). New York: Routledge.

Giroux, H., & McClaren, P. (1989). (Eds.). *Critical pedagogy, the state, and cultural struggle*. Albany, NY: State University of New York Press

Greenberg, M. T., Brown J. L., & Abenavoli, R.M. (2016). *Teacher Stress and Health Effects on Teachers, Students, and Schools*. A report prepared for the Edna Bennett Pierce Prevention Research Center, Pennsylvania State University.. Retrieved from http://www.rwjf.org/content/dam/farm/reports/issue_briefs/2016/rwjf430428

Greenberg, M.T., Weissberg, R.P., Utne O'Brien, M., Zins, J.E., Fredericks, L., & Resnik, H. (2003). Enhancing school-based prevention and youth development through coordinated social, emotional, and academic-learning. *American Psychologist 58,* 451- 466.

Greene, M. (1978). *Landscapes of learning*. New York: Teachers College Press.

Hansen, D. (2005) Creativity in teaching and building a meaningful life as a teacher. *The Journal of Aesthetic Education*, 39(2), 57-68.

Hardy, G. E., Woods, D., & Wall, T. D. (2003). The impact of psychological distress on absence from work. *Journal of Applied Psychology, 83,* 306-314.

Hargreaves, A., & Fink, D. (2006). *Sustainable Leadership*. San Francisco, CA: Jossey- Bass.

Hargreaves, A., & Fullan, M. (2012). *Professional capital: Transforming teaching in every school*. New York: Teachers College Press.

Harris, A., & Muijs, D. (2005). *Improving schools through teacher leadership*. Berkshire, UK: Open University Press.

Hastings, M., & Agrawal, S. (2015). *Lack of teacher engagement linked to 2.3 million missed workdays*. Retrieved from http://www.gallup.com/poll/180455/lack-teacher-engagement-linked-million-missed-workdays.aspx

Heifetz, R., Grashow, A., & Linsky, M. (2009). *The practice of adaptive leadership: Tools and tactics to change your organization and the world.* Boston, MA: Harvard Business Review Press.

Higgins, C. (2011) *The good life of teaching: An ethics of professional practice.* John Wiley & Sons Ltd: UK.

Higgins, C. (2003). Teaching and the good life: A critique of the ascetic ideal in education. *Educational Theory,* 53(2), 131-154.

Inoue, N. (2012). *Mirrors of the mind: Introduction to mindful ways of thinking education.* New York, NY: Peter Lang.

Jennings, P.A., & Greenberg, M. (2009). The pro-social classroom: Teacher social and emotional competence in relation to child and classroom outcomes. *Review of Educational Research,* 79, 491-525.

Jo, Seog Hun. (2014). Teacher commitment: Exploring associations with relationships and emotions. *Teaching and Teacher Education, 43,* 120-130.

Kaser, L., & Halbert, J. (2009). Leadership mindsets: Innovation and learning in the transformation of schools. Routledge, New York, NY.

Kegan, R. (1994). *In over our heads: The mental demands of modern life.* Cambridge, MA: Harvard University Press.

Kegan R., & Wagner, T. (2013). Conclusion. In M. Grogan (Ed.), *The Jossey Bass Reader on Educational Leadership* (3rd ed.) (pp. 220-254). San Francisco, CA: John Wiley & Sons.

Knoop, H. H. (2011). Education in 2025: How positive psychology can revitalize education. In S. Donaldson, M. Csikszentmihalyi, & J. Nakamura (Eds.), *Applied positive psychology: Improving everyday life, health, schools, work and society* (pp. 97–115). New York, NY: Psychology Press.

Koffman, F., & Senge, P. (1993). Communities of commitment: The heart of learning organizations. *Organizational Dynamics,* 22 (2), 5-23.

Kouzes, J., & Posner, B. (1993). *Credibility: How leaders gain it and lose it, why people demand it.* San Francisco, CA: Jossey-Bass.

Kuklthau, C.C., Maniotes, L.K., & Caspari, A.K. (2007). Guided inquiry: Learning in the 21st Century. Westport, CT: Libraries Unlimited.

Kutsyuruba, B., & Walker, K. (2016). High cost of distrust: Restoring trustworthiness in school leadership. In Normore, A., & Brooks, J. (Eds.), *The dark side of leadership: Identifying and overcoming unethical practice in organizations.* Bingley, UK: Emerald.

Kutsyuruba, B., & Walker, K. (2015). The role of trust in developing teacher leaders through early-career induction and mentoring programs. *Antistasis: An Open Educational Journal* (Special Issue on Educational Leadership: Complexities and Practicalities), 5(1), 32-36.

Kutsyuruba, B. & Walker, K. (2014). The lifecycle of trust in educational leadership: An ecological perspective. *International Journal of Leadership in Education.* DOI:10.1080/13603124.2014.915061

Kutsyuruba, B. & Walker, K. (2013). Ethical challenges in school administration: Perspectives of Canadian principals. *Organizational Cultures: An International Journal, 12.*

Kutsyuruba, B., & Walker, K. (2017)(Eds.). *The bliss and blisters of early career teacher: A pan-Canadian perspective.* Burlington, ON: Word and Deed Publications.

Leijon, O., Balliu, N., Lundin, A., Vaez, M., Kjellberg, K., & Hemmingsson, T. (2017). Effects of Psychological Work Factors and Psychological distress on self-assessed work ability: A 7-year follow-up in a general working population. *American Journal of Industrial Medicine, 60*, 121-130.

Lieberman, A., & Mace, D. (2010). Making practice public: Teacher learning in the 21st century. *Journal of Teacher Education, 61* (1-2), 77-88.

Lillius, J. M., Worline, M. C., Dutton, J. E., Kanov, J., Maitlis, S., & Frost, P. J. (2011). Understanding compassion capability, *Human Relations*, 64, 873-899.

Lillius, J.M., Worline, M.C., Maitlis, S. Kanov, J., Dutton, J.E., & Frost, P. (2008). The contours and consequences of compassion at work. Journal of Organizational Behaviour, 29, 193–218.

Lortie, D. C. (1975). *Schoolteacher.* Chicago, IL: The University of Chicago.

Louis, K.S., & Marks, H.M. (1998). Does professional community affect the classroom? Teachers' work and student experiences in restructuring schools. *American Journal of Education*, 106, 532-574.

Lyubomirsky, S. (2007). *The how of happiness: A scientific approach to getting the life you want.* New York, NY: Penguin Books.

Lyubomirsky, S., King, L., & Diener, E. (2005). The benefits of frequent positive affect: Does happiness lead to success? *Psychological Bulletin*, 131(6), 803.

Marks, N. (2011). *The happiness manifesto: How nations and people can nurture wellbeing.* New York: TED Conferences, LLC.

Marzano, R., Waters, T., & Mcnulty, F. (2005). *School leadership that works.* Alexandria, VA: ASCD.

Maslow, A.H. (1943/2013). *A theory of human motivation.* New York: Simon and Schuster.

McGonigal, K. (2015). *The upside of stress: Why stress is good for you, and how to get good at it.* New York, NY: Penguin.

McNiff, J. (2007). My story is my living educational theory. In J. Clandinin (Eds.), *Handbook of Narrative Inquiry: Mapping a Methodology* (pp.308-329).

Mezirow, J. (1991). *Transformative dimensions of adult learning.* San Francisco, CA: Jossey-Bass.

Miller, J. (2007). *The holistic curriculum* (2nd Ed.). Toronto, ON: University of Toronto Press.

Mitchell, C., & Sackney, L. (2009). *Sustainable improvement: Building learning communities that endure.* Rotterdam, Netherlands: Sense.

National Union of Teachers, https://www.teachers.org.uk/news-events/conference-2017/teacher-mental-health-and-wellbeing.

Naylor, C. (2008). *The rising tide of stress in Canada: Time for governments to act in support of schools and society.* Retrieved from https://bctf.ca/uploadedFiles/Publications/Research_reports/2008WLC03.pdf

Nussbaum, M. (2011). *Creating capabilities: The human development approach.* Cambridge, MA: Harvard University Press.

OECD. (2016). *Education at a glance 2016: OECD indicators.* Paris: OECD Publishing. http://dx.doi.org/10.1787/eag-2016-en

Pace, A. (2010). Unleashing positivity in the workplace. *T + D*, 64(1), 40-44.

Peck, S. (1990). *The different drum: Community making and peace.* New York: Arrow Books.

Palmer, P. J. (2009). *A hidden wholeness: The journey toward an undivided life.* Chicago, IL: John Wiley & Sons.

Palmer, P.J. (2007). *The courage to teach: Exploring the inner landscape of a teacher's life* (10th anniversary edition). San Francisco, CA: Jossey-Bass.

Pink, D. (2005). *A whole new mind: Why right-brainers will rule the future.* New York, NY: Penguin Books.

Quinn, R. (2015). *The positive organization: Breaking free from conventional cultures, constraints and beliefs.* Oakland, CA: Berrett-Koehler.

Quinn, R. (2004). *Building the bridge as you walk on it: A guide for leading change*. Oakland, CA: Berrett-Koehler.

Quinn, R. (1996). *Deep change: Discovering the leader within*. Oakland, CA: Berrett-Koehler.

Raelin, J. (2003). *Creating leaderful organizations: How to bring out leadership in everyone*. San Francisco: Berrett-Koehler.

Rassmussen, D. (1999). Human flourishing and the appeal to human nature. *Social Philosophy and Policy*, 16(1), 1-43.

Rath, T. (2006). *Vital friends: The people you can't afford to live without*. New York: Gallup Press

Reed, J. (2007). *Appreciative inquiry: Research for change*. Thousand Oaks, CA: Sage.

Richardson, L. (2000). *Writing: A method of inquiry*. Thousand Oaks, CA: Sage.

Rifkin, J. (2009). *The empathic civilization: The race to global consciousness in a world in crisis*. New York, NY: Penguin Books.

Roset, S., Walker, K., & Cherkowski, S. (2016a). *Flourishing together at Waldheim school*. Saskatoon, SK: Turning Point Global Publishers.

Roset, S., Walker, K., & Cherkowski, S. (2016b). *Rosthern High School: A partnership for success*. Saskatoon, SK: Turning Point Global Publishers.

Roset, S., Walker, K., & Cherkowski, S. (2016c). *Langham Elementary School: Growing, learning, sharing, Caring*. Saskatoon, SK: Turning Point Global Publishers.

Roset, S., Walker, K., Cherkowski, S., & Wilson, J. (2017). *Sunwest: Empowering 21st century learners*. Saskatoon, SK: Turning Point Global Publishers.

Sackney, L., & Walker, K. (2007). Sustainable innovation in exemplary schools. *International Journal of Interdisciplinary Social Sciences,* 1, 1-10.

Sanga, K., & Walker, K. (2011). Mentoring by questions. In E. Ralph & K. Walker (Eds.). *Adapting mentorship across the professions: Fresh insights and perspectives* (pp. 269-290), Calgary: Detselig Enterprises Ltd.

Scharmer, O. (2009). *Theory U: Leading from the future as it emerges*. Oakland, CA: Berrett-Koehler.

Scharmer, O., & Kaufer, K. (2013). *Leading from the emerging future: From ego-system to eco-system economies*. Oakland, CA: Berrett-Koehler.

Scheffler, I. (1985). *Of human potential: An essay in the philosophy of education.* Boston, MA: Routledge & Kegan Paul.

Sackney, L., Walker, K., & Mitchell, C. (2005). Building capacity for learning communities: Schools that work. *REICE, 3*(1), 9-16.

Sackney, L., & Walker, K. (2007). Sustainable innovation in exemplary schools. *International Journal of Interdisciplinary Social Sciences,* 1, 1-10.

Schonert-Reichl, K., & Hymel, S. (2007). Educating the heart as well as the mind: Social and Emotional Learning for School and Life Success. *Education Canada,* 47(2), 20-25.

Seligman, M. (2011). *Flourish: A visionary new understanding of happiness and wellbeing.* New York, NY: Free Press.

Seligman, M. (2002). *Authentic happiness: Using the new positive psychology to realize your potential for lasting fulfillment.* New York, NY: Free Press.

Seligman, M., & Csikszentmihalyi, M. (2000). Positive psychology: An introduction. *American Psychologist,* 55(1), 5-14.

Seligman, M., Ernst, R., Gillham, J., Reivich, K., & Linkins, M. (2009). Positive education: Positive psychology and classroom interventions. *Oxford Review of Education,* 35, 293–311.

Sen, A. (2009). *The idea of justice.* London: Allen Lane.

Senge, P. (2006). *The fifth discipline: The art and practice of the learning organization* (2nd Ed.). New York, NY: Crown Publishing Group.

Senge, P., Smith, B., Kruschwitz, N., Laur, J., & Schley, S. (2008*). The necessary revolution: How individuals and organizations are working together to create a sustainable world.* New York, NY: Doubleday.

Sergiovanni, T.S. (2005). The virtues of leadership. *The Educational Forum, 66* (Winter), 112-123.

Sergiovanni, T. (1996). *Moral leadership: Getting to the heart of school improvement.* San Francisco, CA: Jossey Bass.

Sergiovanni, T.J. (1994). Organizations or communities? Changing the metaphor changes the theory. *Educational Administration Quarterly,* 30(2), 214-220.

Sharma, R. (2010). *The leader who had no title: A modern fable on real success in business and in life.* New York, NY: Simon and Schuster.

Skaalvik, E., & Skaalvik, S. (2009). Does school context matter? Relations with teacher burnout and job satisfaction. *Teacher and Teacher Education, 25,* 518-524.

Skaalvik, E., & Skaalvik, S. (2007). Dimensions of teacher self-efficacy and relations with strain factors, perceived collective teacher efficacy, and teacher burnout. *Journal of Educational Pyschology, 99* (3), 611-625.

Slater, L. (2008). Pathways to building leadership capacity. *Educational Management, Administration, and Leadership*, 36(1) 55-69.

Starratt, R. (2012). *Cultivating an ethical school.* London, UK: Routledge.

Starratt, R. J. (2011). *Refocusing school leadership: Foregrounding human development throughout the work of the school.* New York, NY: Routledge.

Starratt, R. (2003). *Centering Educational administration: Cultivating meaning, community and moral responsibility*. Mahwah, NJ: Lawrence Erlbaum Associates.

Stephens, J.P., Heaphy, E.D., Carmeli, A., Spreitzer, G.M., & Dutton, J.E. (2013). Relationship quality and virtuousness: Emotional carrying capacity as a source of individual and team resilience, *Journal of Applied Behavioral Science*, 49(1), 13-41.

Stoll, L., & Louis, K.S. (2007). (Eds). *Professional learning communities: Divergence, depth and dilemmas.* Berkshire, UK: Open University Press.

Tschannen-Moran, M. (2004). *Trust matters: Leadership for successful schools.* San Francisco, CA: Jossey-Bass.

United Nations Educational, Scientific and Cultural Organization (2015). *Rethinking education: Towards a global common good?* Paris: UNESCO. Retrieved from http://unescodoc.unesco.org/images/0023/002325/232555e.pdf

Vanier, J. (2008). *Becoming human*. Toronto, ON: House of Anansi Press.

Vanier, J. (2003). *Finding peace.* Toronto, ON: House of Anansi Press.

Walker, K. (2006). Fostering hope: A leaders first and last task. *Journal of Educational Administration*, 44(6), 540-569.

Walker, K., Noonan, B., & Kutsyuruba, B. (2011). The fragility of trust in the world of school principals. *Journal of Educational Administration*, 49(5), 471-494.

Weick, K. (1995). *Sensemaking in organizations.* London, UK: Sage.

Wenger, E. (1998). *Communities of practice, learning, meaning and identity.* Cambridge, MA: Cambridge University Press.

Williams, M., Teasdale, J., Segal, Z., & Kabat-Zinn, J. (2007). *The mindful way through depression: Freeing yourself from chronic unhappiness.* New York, NY: The Guildford Press.

Wheatley, M. (2012). *So far from home: Lost and found in a brave new world.* Oakland, CA: Berrett-Koehler.

Wheatley, M. (2005). *Finding our way: Leadership for an uncertain time.* Oakland, CA: Berrett-Koehler.

Wheatley, M. (1999). *Leadership and the new science: Learning about organization from an orderly universe.* Oakland, CA: Berrett-Koehler.

Whitehead, J. (2008). Using a living theory methodology in improving practice generating educational knowledge in living theories. *Electronic Journal of Living Theories,* 1(1),103-126.

Whitney, D., & Trosten-Bloom, A. (2010). *The power of appreciative inquiry: A practical guide to positive change.* (2nd Ed.). Oakland, CA: Berrett-Koehler.

Zins, J., Weissberg, R., Wang, M., & Walberg, H. J. (2004). (Eds.). *Building academic success on social and emotional learning: What does the research say?* New York, NY: Teacher's College Press.

Your Learning Companions: Sabre and Keith

Sabre is an Associate Professor and Director of the Centre for Mindful Engagement at the University of British Columbia. She teaches and researches in the areas of leadership and organizational development, with a current focus on wellbeing; professional learning and collaboration; mentoring and coaching; and diversity and education. She brings her experiences as a teacher, coach and parent to her passion for exploring flourishing in educational contexts.

Keith is a Professor in the Department of Educational Administration at the University of Saskatchewan. His recognized areas of work include educational governance and policy-making, leadership and organizational development and capacity-building, together with applied and professional ethics. He brings over 40 years of experience as a manager, teacher, minister, leader, scholar and educational administrator in public and social sectors.

Manufactured by Amazon.ca
Bolton, ON

34117600R00101